*After Midnight
In Savannah*

"Emerson would get fed up. Time and time again, he'd come to our house and say, 'They're at it again. Sooner or later, one's going to kill the other.' This was probably two years before . . . ."

All statements in this book are taken from personal interviews, correspondence and/or court transcripts.

Copyright © 2005 by B. Forrest Spink. All rights reserved. No part of this book may be reproduced, stored or transmitted in any form or by any means without written permission from B. Forrest Spink and/or ThomasMax Publishing.

Poetry in the Appendix A copyright © by James Mize Martin. Publication credits as listed with the poetry.

Family photographs courtesy of Barbara Perry.

Midnight In The Garden of Good And Evil, © 1994 by John Berendt, published in the U.S.A. by Vantage Books, a division of Random House, Inc.

Fatal Flowers copyright © 1980 by Rosemary Daniell. Originally published in the U.S.A. by Holt, Rinehart and Winston. Current reprint rights are held by Hill Street Press.

Cover photo of Alva Martin courtesy of Barbara Perry.

Cover photo depicting strangulation marks courtesy of and used with permission from Erika Killen, with special make-up effects by Erika Killen.

First printing, May 2005.

ThomasMax Publishing
P.O. Box 250054
Atlanta, GA 30325
thomasmax.com

For those who have encouraged my writing, initially Sam R. and Barbara, and to Robert, for all of his encouragement

On New Year's Day, 1991, James Mize Martin, then thirty-four years old, had two living parents, a roof over his head that belonged to him, and a partner in a relationship. He was unemployed at the time, but by March, 1991, he would have a job.

"I was in my trailer, alone with my cats and the TV," Martin recalled when asked about his last change-of-year holiday outside of prison walls. "Dad and Mom were in the house doing whatever they were doing, probably sleeping. I don't remember exactly how I spent (New Year's Eve), but I imagine I went to sleep by ten or eleven."

"My trailer" was a camper-trailer that he had purchased several years earlier. It was parked in the back yard of the home of his parents, Emerson and Alva Martin.

On New Year's Day, 1992, James Mize Martin sat in a jail cell. Both of his parents were dead. His partner would have no contact with him. His job had been lost.

His father died in September after open-heart surgery. In less than seven months, he quit the job he had started in March. In December, his mother was murdered. After James Mize Martin was arrested for her murder, his relationship partner refused any further contact or communication.

So what happened in that year that spun Martin's life into a free-falling downward spiral? In a nutshell, two words: crack cocaine. Jim Martin met the drug in May of 1991. While the death of his father shortly thereafter was coincidental, crack cocaine proved to be the ruination of Jim's life on every other front. It caused the death of his mother. In 1993, he was convicted of her murder.

It appeared to be an open-and-shut case. The "crackhead son" had run out of things of his own to sell to finance his drug habit, so he killed his recently widowed mother so that he could sell her things, too. And he had other reasons to want her dead. He had stolen and used her credit cards, for which he had received a sentence of probation. That probation was about to be revoked, and his mother would have been the primary witness at his revocation hearing. And he made no secret that he resented what his mother stood for as a Nazarene minister.

Of course, the "crackhead son" pleaded not guilty and maintained that he had not done it. But, then, in prison, almost all inmates maintain their innocence . . . that they are there only because they had lousy lawyers.

James Mize Martin was that "crackhead son" whose mother, Alva, was murdered in December of 1991 at her home in Savannah, Georgia. However, more than decade later, he maintains that he did not kill his mother. While that may not seem unusual, what *is* unusual is that he does not argue that he deserves to be incarcerated. In fact, he claims that being arrested and jailed probably saved his life by depriving him of the drug that stole not only much of his life, but which also ultimately led to his mother's death.

In a society in which unusual behavior

garners headlines, Jim Martin stands tall. In some ways, he makes guests of Jerry Springer on television look like *The Brady Bunch*. Although it's been many years since Martin's conviction, Owen Ferguson, the officer to whom Martin was turned over on the fateful night of his arrest, remembers it as clearly as a horror movie. In particular, the horror movie, *Psycho*.

"Every time I remember it, I think of the Bates Motel," Ferguson said.

Virtually everyone involved in the case, from Ferguson to the jury that convicted Martin, would agree that Jim Martin killed Alva Martin as the climax of a horrid series of events which centered around her son's use of crack cocaine. There are two dissenters: Jim Martin himself, who claims the murderer was a man named Larry Smith, and Martin's aunt, Barbara Perry, sister-in-law of Alva Martin.

Perry, however, doesn't maintain that her nephew is innocent. On the contrary, the first thing she said when interviewed at her rural Georgia home was, "I believe he did it." However, her opinion is that Jim would have killed Alva at some point, with or without crack cocaine . . . or any other drugs . . . being involved. Their relationship, the core of the dysfunctional Martin family, is what differentiates this story from other gruesome drug-related murders.

There are other sidelines to the tale.

First of all, Jim Martin is not your stereotypical crackhead. He is Caucasian. He did not come from poverty, but from a middle-class upbringing. He is intelligent and educated. A prison I.Q. test in 1994 measured his intelligence quotient to be 130, well above average.

One of the most immortalized murder trials in recent history also came out of Savannah. That story of Jim Williams is told in John Berendt's *Midnight In The Garden of Good And Evil*. Jim Martin knew Jim Williams. He had been to one of Williams' famous Christmas parties. The Martins, however, lived a long way, socially speaking, from Savannah's famed Historic District (although just a few minutes away by car). Their home was in Bona Bella, on the eastern outskirts of Savannah, not quite an impoverished zone, but a far cry from the homes built with old money in the Historic District . . . homes which, it is said, made Savannah "too beautiful to burn" in the eyes of Civil War General William Tecumseh Sherman. (See Appendix F for more detail about the neighborhood of Bona Bella)

Enhancing the flavor of the story is Larry Smith, who admitted in court that he had repeatedly supplied Jim Martin with crack cocaine. Smith, about thirty-six years of age (he testified to being thirty-seven during the trial in February of 1993) at the time of the murder, was better known in Savannah as a cross-dresser named Latrice Boudair, sometimes spelled Boudoir. Rosemary Daniell's *Fatal Flowers*, an autobiographical story of "sin, sex and suicide in the deep south" (so states the jacket to the book), includes references to Boudair. "A fascinating character," Ms. Daniell recalled in recent correspondence with this writer.

Adding further spice to the plot, the dead body of Alva Martin was stored in a closet for more than week before being discovered. Meanwhile, her son attempted to imitate his mother's voice on the telephone in hopes of making others believe that she was still alive. Some were fooled. Longtime neighbors, however, testified in court that they knew they had been talking to Jim, not Alva.

The story made front-page headlines in the local newspapers. The headlines began in the *Savannah Evening Press* the day after Alva Martin's body was discovered. Man Held In Death Of Mother appeared in the left-hand column on page one of that day's 40-page edition. The headlines continued as information came in that Alva had been strangled, and the trial made daily headlines in both the evening paper and the *Savannah Morning News*.

At the time that this book went to press in May, 2005, James Mize Martin was serving a life sentence for the murder of his mother at Johnson State Prison in Wrightsville, Georgia. He was held in Chatham County Jail between the time of his arrest in December, 1991, until his trial, in February, 1993. He has been moved around through various facilities in the Georgia Department of Corrections system since that time, including stops at Phillips State Prison in Buford, Rutledge State Prison in Columbus, Central State Prison in Macon and privately-run Coffee Correctional Institute in Nicholls before being transferred to Johnson in 2004. He was denied parole in 1998. His next parole hearing is scheduled for 2006.

How Do You Smell Dysfunction?

The Martin family epitomized "dysfunction," a buzzword in today's psychology-laden world. Jim Martin, who has had a lot of psychological therapy since being incarcerated in late 1991, recognized the degree of strangeness in his own family. Much of it is evident in his poems (see Appendix A), one of which is titled, "How Do You Smell Dysfunction?"

According to accounts by his son, Jim, and his sister, Barbara Perry, Emerson Martin was born in 1920 at Fort Screven Hospital on Tybee Island. Fort Screven was at that time an active military base under the command of General George C. Marshall, who would later be immortalized by his Marshall Plan. Emerson was named after Ralph Waldo Emerson.

Emerson served in World War II. He had two children by Betsey, his first wife. The children were Bettie and Emerson Jr., known to family members as Buddy. Buddy is now deceased. At the time Emerson and Alva were married, Bettie and Buddy were ten and nine, respectively.

By all accounts, Emerson was a likeable man. "Everybody liked Big Em," his sister Barbara recalls.

He was also relatively successful in carving

out a decent living for his family. Although he had only a ninth-grade education, Emerson served as a civil engineer for 37 years. "My daddy was my best friend," Jim Martin commented. "There wasn't anything he couldn't do or make happen. He had a garden that we ate fresh vegetables out of practically year-round. At church, he was Sunday School Superintendent, Choir Director, taught a Sunday School class, was head usher, and he was on the Board of Trustees.

"I spent as much time with him as I was allowed. He always knew what to do in every situation. He never let me down in any way. I'm alive today because of him. He was very affectionate, warm, loving. He smelled like Old Spice . . . occasionally like English Leather."

Alva Virginia Mize was born June 20, 1916, in Atlanta, the last of six children. Like her husband Emerson, she was also named for a famous person, inventor Thomas Alva Edison. According to Jim Martin, his mother's family branches into both famous and infamous waters.

"We are related to folks like Johnny Mize," he said, referring to the baseball Hall of Fame member. "His nickname was 'The Big Cat.' This was when Andres Gallaraga's family was still in Cuba. (Gallaraga was also known by that nickname throughout a successful baseball career which ended in 2004.) I've always hated it that they gave (Gallaraga) my cousin's nickname, but that's just the Mize in me talking."

While Johnny Mize and pro golfer Larry Mize make for an impressive pedigree on one side, Jim Martin points to a darker side to the family as well.

"There were Mize cousins who went out west. One of the men abused his wife and finally killed her . . . and got away with it. We had some pictures of them from the 1890's and early 1900's, and they looked like outlaws. They make the James Gang look like a bunch of Jesuit fathers.

"And (also there was) Chuck Mize, the coach in Atlanta, who was killed by his son a few years back. The boy also stabbed the mother about seventeen times, but she lived. They're cousins, too."

Jim pulls no punches in describing his opinion of his maternal lineage. "The Mizes have always been so holier than thou, so sanctimonious, so pious, so perfect, their shit smells like rose petals."

At the time Emerson and Alva met, he lived in Savannah, and she lived in Atlanta. Virtually every day he wrote love letters to her (airmail postage was six cents in 1954). As early as September, just a couple months after they had first met, his letters contained phrases such as, "Darling Angel, I want to make you the happiest wife in the world."

They were married in December.

"The way it sounded to me, I thought he married awfully soon," Barbara Perry said. "Emerson's first wife died in June of 1954. We went to church camp meeting in July. He met Alva there and they started corresponding. By December, they were married. At the time, I was really upset. I felt it was too soon. But he said everybody had said she was a fine, upstanding Christian lady, and that she'd be able to help him with the children."

If caring for Bettie and Buddy was the motivation for Emerson Martin to marry Alva Mize, he would very soon be bitterly disappointed. Immediately after they were married, Alva advised her husband that she would only be able to take care of one of his children. Bettie, who had been staying with the Perrys most of the time, was dispatched there on a full-time basis, leaving only Emerson's namesake to be raised by the new couple. It brought the Perry household to five members. Robert Perry had two sons, Gordon and Mike, from his first marriage. Robert's first wife had died when his sons were very young. He married Barbara about five years later. Emerson, however, wasn't willing to wait that long.

"I don't think Emerson had any idea what he was in for. When I questioned him, he said that he felt he couldn't raise the children by himself. But, of course, she (Alva) didn't do that. I don't think he felt that she would put his children out. He told me he was lonely, but he made a mistake. Betsey had cooked three meals a day, washed, ironed, starched his uniforms for the National Guard, all that kind of stuff. Alva, if she cooked, she had to go to the grocery store every day. She did not buy for but one day, for the meal she was going to cook. She didn't do the laundry; it had to be sent out. She did none of the housework. That was unheard of."

With only one child, it seemed that maybe the new couple would be able to settle in. Buddy, however, raised Alva's ire with his behavioral problems.

"She said she couldn't control him, so she packed his bags and put him out," Barbara Perry recalled. "About that time he was 11 or 12 years old."

"Out" meant out on the front steps. The door was locked behind him. With nowhere else to go, Buddy sought refuge with his sister at the Perry household.

"We took him," Barbara said. "We kept him as long as we could, but he was in and out of prison probably over half of his life. And his only crime was shoplifting. He was a kleptomaniac."

Barbara Perry says it was Alva's intention to get rid of both of Emerson's children from the start.

"She didn't want him (Buddy). And when they finally had Jim (who was born in August, 1956), it was 'us three and no more.' They would come to our place every year for Thanksgiving, but at Christmas time, she would always say to me, 'This is our family time, so we want just the three of us.'"

"Bettie and Buddy were not allowed to call her 'Mom,' 'Mama,' 'Mother' or even 'Stepmom.' Only 'Alva.' I was only allowed to call her 'Mother.' She didn't respond to anything else," Jim recalled.

Alva did give Bettie a "Sweet Sixteen" birthday party and also hosted a wedding shower for Emerson's daughter. "But she (Alva) complained," Jim said, "that after all she did for my sister, she (Bettie) didn't appreciate anything.

"I don't remember anything she did for Buddy. He was in and out of the juvenile home and did time at Reidsville in the 60's and 70's. So, of course, any contact with him was severely limited."

Although they were only "half" siblings, Jim said, "I never thought of them as anything but my brother and sister. I never thought of them as half of anything. I guess I was closer to Bettie, even though Buddy could have certainly taught me a lot. Bettie and I were never allowed to have the kind of relationship I always wanted. When I was growing up, I used to pretend and fantasize that I was Bettie's or Barbara's child. They were both so beautiful."

Bettie's life turned out to be tragic.

"The girl's had the worst life of anybody you could ever imagine," Barbara Perry said. "Emerson didn't treat her right. Alva didn't treat her right. She married a man who was supposedly a minister, and they had four children, and then he ran off with another woman. The first child (deceased in 2004) was born with eye cancer, which left her blind, and she has a child that's blind. A granddaughter ran away from home, left with a drug dealer. One of her sons was in prison for statutory rape. Another one dealt drugs, but he's straightened up now."

In addition to purging her step-children, Alva was also intent on erasing the memory of their mother. "No one was allowed to mention Betsey's name in my mother's presence," Jim said. Alva didn't even use the name herself, preferring to call a cousin named Betsy Ricks Hardy by "Betty" rather than her given name.

Her attitudes and behavior seem enigmatic to her chosen role as a woman of God. Alva was Reverend Alva, a Nazarene minister.

"She loved being called Reverend Alva," Barbara Perry said. "I've never known anybody else like her. In some ways she was very good and kind, and she did a lot of volunteer work in the nursing homes. But yet, there was another side. She lived for her ministry. That was her priority, not Jimmy and Emerson." (See Appendix B for one of her sermons.)

Until the late 1960's, Alva's mother, Dovie Lou Mize, visited the Martins for three months out of the year. On one other occasion, Jim Martin said, some other members of the Mize family spent one or two nights with them.

"My mother's mother was an absolute saint, the kindest person I've ever known," Jim recalled. "But she had to be. None of her children had her sweet, long-suffering disposition."

Frequently, the Martins would visit Alva's relatives in the Atlanta area. When visiting Mize family members, Alva had strict rules for her husband and son.

"My mother was ashamed of her house and her reduced living circumstances," Jim said. "All the family knew was what she told them, or what they were able to infer from the many visits we made to Atlanta, Stone Mountain, Decatur, Conley and Augusta over the years. My daddy and I were dressed 'just so' and put on our best behavior. Mother was huge on the appearance. Even people in Savannah only knew us as this perfect façade of a family."

The façade never fooled Barbara Perry, or her husband, Robert.

"She was inconsiderate, overbearing," Robert noted. "She could be a nice person, but it was Alva or nothing. Her ideas were number one. She was overbearing on her son. He had to play in the yard by himself. He had no visitors. He had a bicycle, but he could ride it in the yard; he couldn't go out on the street. And this was all the way up (into adolescence)."

"He (Jim) was smothered," Barbara said. "He wasn't mothered. He never had a life. Really, it was just church, and that was it. No music unless it was religious music. Of course, the church we went to (Nazarene, an extremely conservative branch of Protestant Christianity), we didn't dance or go to movies or anything like that, so he had nothing except church. And he was required to go every time. Plus she did a lot of volunteer work. She had (church) services at about five nursing homes every week, and he had to there, too.

"And this was not just before he went to school. It was all the way up into his teen years. Where she went, he had to go. He was tied to her apron strings, and she wasn't going to cut loose."

Her son wasn't the only one affected by Alva's domineering behavior. Emerson Martin's life was radically changed, too.

"He was pretty much that way (tied to Alva's apron strings), too," Barbara said. "The last few months (before dying in 1991), he came to see us. He said, 'If I was younger, I'd start all over again. I'd leave. But with my age and my health, I can't leave. But life is hell.'"

Alva also discouraged Emerson from visiting his own mother. "Alva was insanely jealous. She didn't want Emerson to have any contact with my (and his) mother. She didn't want him to have affection for Mother, and he was really the closest to Mother of the three of us (children)."

Emerson did, however, visit his mother often, so Jim had plenty of opportunities to visit with his paternal grandmother.

"Jim loved Mama," Barbara said. "Mama was a strange one, too. She wanted her way. But Alva, the jealousy with mother was just . . . well, when Emerson came over to see Mom, which he did, once a week in addition to seeing her at church services, Alva would call. Emerson wouldn't be there five minutes before she called, asking, 'Where are you? What are you doing? When are you coming home?' After Mom died, Emerson came to see us (Robert and Barbara) about once a week, and she'd always call. She always had a reason . . . like telling him to stop and pick up this or that at the store."

Alva was determined to make her son a star performer in church. It was, Jim says, the case of a would-be stage mother living vicariously through her child. Alva's dream was for Jim to become a star evangelist/singer who traveled the globe to win souls for Jesus. The preparation began when he was barely toilet trained.

"That started when I was two years old," Jim said. "It was at a Christmas program of some sort at my mom's church. I had to stand up in front of the church. I think they hitched me up on the altar rail or something. I was very afraid. I was scared to death. I had done a lot of stuff at home, but it's different when you show out at home, and I was really scared.

"I remember having to go to the bathroom, so I told my Mom, and she said, 'Well, if you still have to go to the bathroom when this is over, you can go then.'" With a smile, he added, "From that day to this one, I can hold it a long time. That can be an asset in prison. This is a hurry up and wait kind of place, kind of like, 'We wanted you an hour ago, but stand here for forty-five minutes.'"

All throughout his young life, Jim was forced to perform. Although church was his primary stage, his mother was a Shirley Temple fan, and he was encouraged to perform at-home song-and-dance routines to "Good Ship Lollipop" and "Animal Crackers In My Soup."

Dressed as Shirley Temple?

"Well, that's kind of androgynous thing isn't it?" he said. "Here I was in a little sailor suit with short pants and big curly hair. My hair was blond as a child. When I was twelve or thirteen, it started getting darker. Believe it or not, to this day, I still know almost all of Shirley Temple's songs, and I can sing and dance all the routines she did in the movies."

Alva's pressure on Jim to perform led to resentment at an early age.

"I started resenting it when I was maybe five or six. I matured very early." He laughed, then continued, "I began having sex when I was seven years old because I wanted to. That says a lot."

Psychologists would have had a field day with young Jimmy Martin's domineering mother and his early start into homosexuality.

"My folks and I would go out to eat on Friday night in downtown Savannah. Levy's Department Store had a dining room there, and my mom had an account at the store, so we'd go there and eat. I'd leave them and go off to use the bathroom. I was a smart little kid. I was reading on a real high level and understood a lot of things that a lot of little kids didn't understand. When I went into first grade and they tested me, I was reading on a sixth-grade level. And they have all these kinds of things written on the walls of the bathrooms, and I wanted to find out how I could get involved in this."

Did the boy who could read far beyond his years understand what he was reading on the walls?

"Those things don't leave much to the imagination. I had a pretty good idea of what the writing on the walls meant. So, pretty much every week, I'd be down there having sex. It was always with a different stranger. I don't think any of them ever came back the following week."

He recalled his first experience.

"I was in a stall, and I left the door open. Somebody finally walked into the stall. He walked up to where I was sitting, and he said, 'Have you ever licked a peppermint stick?' That stands out in my memory, you know? And he says, 'Well, lick this,' and I did. He was erect, and, to me, it was just massive. I remember he came all over the wall back behind me, and I remember looking at him and down at myself and wondering, 'Wow, will this ever happen to me?'"

The theory of the link between the domineering mother and homosexuality gets support from Barbara Perry in this case. "I think she (Alva) contributed (to Jim's homosexuality). I knew from an early age that he was gay, but I accepted him as that. That's Jimmy."

Jim Martin, however, disputes his mother's influence as the determining factor.

"I think I was born gay," he said. "I think a number of people are. I can remember being four, five, six years old. Growing up in Savannah, a beach town, I was attracted to guys with their shirts off. That was the first thing that caught my attention.

"My mom said the first thing that attracted me as a baby was women's lipstick. A lot of people wanted to hold me, and I would try to grab their lips. Red lipstick was my favorite color. Red was my mother's favorite color, so I guess, ergo, it became mine, too."

One of his earliest memories is one of makeshift cross-dressing.

"I was three years old, and we had just moved to Savannah. The garment bags that you get from the laundry . . . I tore a couple holes in either side and put a belt on it. I didn't have anything on underneath it. I guess I didn't know much about foundation garments then," he said, laughing. "I put on some high heels, grabbed a pocketbook and was out the door, down the drive when Mother came running out there. I told her, 'Bye, I'm going to the store.'"

Growing up as the gay son of a Nazarene preacher-woman and her passive husband was a challenge. In spite of his resentment of his mother, Martin says he loved his mother "very much, but I was scared to death of her, too."

His father, he said, was his best friend.

"I was really Daddy's boy. We did guy things, like play ball in the backyard, but I wasn't allowed to participate in things at school. No Boy Scouts, no Cub Scouts, no softball, no Little League."

Alva wouldn't allow such affiliations. "Religion was her top priority," Barbara Perry explained. "Everything else came second. While

Jim was growing up, he wasn't allowed to have friends. He had to stay right with her. Emerson wasn't really allowed to take him to ball games or stuff like that, because she felt like that was wrong. Em loved sports. He was very outgoing, happy-go-lucky, but she changed all that."

Given his extraordinary reading level, it was somewhat surprising that Jim did not excel in school. The problem was centered around his attention span, which resulted in a recommendation that he be sent to a special school.

"I did pretty good, somewhere around a B-plus. I remember after taking an IQ test that three different moms and dads were asked to bring their children to school for a conference. The principal wanted to put me in a special school. The closest one was in Atlanta then, and my mom wouldn't send me away from home to go to this school. It probably would have made all the difference in my life, because I was a kid that needed special attention that I wasn't going to get in a public school. And so I was constantly doing things to get attention. I spent a lot of time in the principal's office."

Divided attention contributed to his lack of academic excellence, too.

"I was so many different people at an early age," he explained. "I had to be Mom's little whatever, I had to be the perfect little church kid, I was sneaking around whenever I could and going to a public bathroom, and I was balancing all this stuff out. It was difficult for me to fit in with other kids."

What might have happened if he had been sent to the school in Atlanta?

"I would have gotten a lot better education,

and I think I might have really done something with performing and art more than I was able to do. I wasn't allowed to perform what I wanted to perform."

Psychologists probing deeper into Jim Martin's upbringing would also have a field day with the fact that he developed into a sexually passive masochist after enduring regular whippings as a child.

"My mom whipped me most every day of my life until I was twelve. Then she decided I was too old to be whipped, so she punished me in other ways, like putting me in a closet for an hour or so, or sending me to bed without supper."

Alva's punishment weapon of choice was usually a tree limb, although Jim also remembers being beaten with belts, paddles and rulers.

"A lot of the time, she would go outside and get a branch and bring it in and whip me with that."

Were the whippings deserved, most of the time, anyway?

"I don't think so," he said, laughing. "I'll give you an example. In first grade, we were divided up into tables, and each table was going to do a little entertainment thing for the class. My mom knew about this, and she wanted me to go to school with all these kids who were not religious fanatics and get up in front of them and sing *The Old Rugged Cross*. But I didn't want to do that, so I got up and did the twist with the rest of the kids. My mother found about it, because I lied to her when I got home. I'd told her how much the kids had loved *The Old Rugged Cross*, that it was the hit of the show. My mom called the teacher. That's how she was.

And I got whipped."

"I don't doubt that she beat him," Barbara Perry said. "If he stepped to the side, she probably did, because that took him out of her path. I wasn't aware of any beatings, but she did enough to restrict him without that. The whole thing bothered me, the way that she treated him and gave him no freedom. Robert and I talked about it, and we'd concluded that once Jimmy got loose, he was going to go wild. I'm sure she loved him, but it was a strange love."

"My father tried to intervene a lot for me," Jim said. "He tried to talk to her, but it had no effect."

Never, however, Jim said, did he confront Alva by trying to hit her back, or even by shouting at her.

"The course my resentment took was in rebellion . . . personal rebellion, so everything she wanted me to do, I would do something different than that. I did it behind her back, and I usually got caught. That's why I got all those whippings."

Alva, however, never knew about the elementary school boy running amok in public restrooms.

"She didn't know about that. By the time I was an adult, she probably had some idea, but I don't know that she ever knew. She absolutely never knew about my wilder side and my masochism."

There was, however, one incident during his childhood that got Alva's attention. That event led her to admit to some of her own past.

"She had a talk with me when I was eleven or twelve, when I was messing with another little boy down the street. She said she had slept with women who had received satisfaction from it, but she never got anything out of it. She said it was wrong, it didn't lead to marriage, and it could ruin your life."

Her son's use of drugs ultimately led to Alva Martin's murder. Ironically, Jim says, he was introduced to drugs by his mother. The point was raised during the trial, but Martin's testimony about drugs as a child was rendered more or less useless to the jury when Barbara Perry was recalled and said it would have been against Alva's nature to use prescription drugs on a widespread basis.

When interviewed more than a decade after Alva's murder, however, Jim Martin says that his mother, did, indeed, introduce him to "better living through chemistry."

He said, "I started taking drugs when I was six. My mother started giving me tranquilizers. I was a hyperactive kid, so she thought nothing of giving me some. There was never anything in my life about going to a doctor or about therapy. To her, there was only one physician who was The Great Physician, and He (God) was going to take care of everybody's problems. But, in the meantime, if my mom needed help going to sleep at night, which she did every day of her life, she got something from the doctor . . . or from the druggist, illegally, but never mind that story. Then she started giving it to me.

"In about 1974, before I moved to Atlanta, my dad had a mild heart attack, and at that time, his doctor gave him Quaaludes, Seconals and Demerol. He gave some of those to my mother and me. So that's really how I started taking drugs. I never had any moral reservations about trying drugs after that."

Until he was introduced to crack cocaine, Martin says he had no problems balancing his life and his drugs.

"I never felt like I had to have a Quaalude or a joint. I started smoking pot in college . . . the community college. I went out to lunch with this group of girls, and they said, 'Hey, let's smoke a joint.' I never had done it, but I did. I was seventeen at the time. It was great. I went back to class, but I giggled so much that I had to leave class that day."

At age 18, Jim Martin left the local community college and moved to Atlanta.

"I wanted to move. I was 18. It was legal. They (my parents) couldn't stop me. They didn't really try, but they wanted me to finish at the local community college. I wanted to explore myself more than I could do in Savannah."

"To explore myself" included to branch out sexually, too. He was no longer the child that was lurking in bathrooms; he wanted to explore some of the kinkier facets of his sexual desires, something he felt would be more accessible in a larger city.

"I wanted to go and get a job and live in Atlanta. My mom was from there, and I was very familiar with it. In Savannah, I felt like I was a big fish in a little pond, and I wanted to be a big fish in a big pond."

For a while, things went well for him in Atlanta. He worked at Music City (a now-defunct record store), for an insurance company, for Dean Witter Brokerage, for First National Bank of Atlanta, and in the medical records department at Crawford Long Hospital. Most of the jobs were of short duration. The job with Dean Witter was the longest stint, approximately 18 months. He also worked as a female impersonator in an Atlanta nightclub. The money wasn't great from any of the jobs, but, for the most part, he says he was happy. Then, in 1980, he decided to return to Savannah.

"My apartment was broken into, and I was really afraid for the first time in my life," he explained. "Before the burglary, there were a lot of calls and hang-ups. Maybe they were just setting me up. It was really strange, because my best friend from Savannah had just been there, and he was about to break up with his lover, so he had left a lot of jewelry with me. I had a big raccoon fur coat that I wore. It was stolen. All his jewelry was stolen. And I'll always think that my friend's lover had something to do with it . . . that he wanted him back and he wanted to get the stuff that had been left with me."

Barbara Perry tells about the circumstances that prompted Jim's return a little differently. "I heard he was prostituting himself in Atlanta," she said. "That's very dangerous. The lifestyle he was living could very easily have killed him. I don't know everything that went on in Atlanta, but Emerson had to go and get him and bail him out of whatever trouble he was in."

Regardless of the motivation, everyone agrees that Emerson and Alva Martin welcomed their son back home with open arms. "They were happy to have me back. My dad had never wanted me to leave, and he was just overjoyed. He always told me not to believe that crap about, 'you can't come home again,' and that I always had a home there.

"I paid for my trailer, and I also paid some on the utility bills to help them out. Plus I paid my own phone bills."

And so began, for the most part, a peaceful era in the relationship of the Martin family . . . more or less a decade of calm before the final storm.

The Year of Tragedy

In February of 1981, shortly after his return to Savannah, Jim got a job at Candler Medical Records.

"My mom went in and talked to the woman who was the administrator. Her name was Virginia Daniel. I worked with her for five or six years at the hospital. She knew me and knew the relationship I had with my mother. At my trial, the man I worked for the last six months claimed that my mother and I had terrible fights on the phone and stuff like that, and it's not true. Virginia knew me, and she would say she never saw any signs of that."

Ms. Daniel retired in 1986, and Jim Martin and his new boss "never got along that well." Finally, in late 1988, he resigned. In 1989, he took a job with a loan company. He worked there for nine months.

Between the two jobs, he took some time off and, for the first time in his life, became involved in a relationship with another man.

"After I left the hospital, this buddy of mine that I'd been buying the pot from for years said, 'Hey, don't work for a while, just hang out with me. I've got plenty of money, and you've spent all this money with me over all these years. Let me do this for you now. Let's have some fun.' So that's what we did. We'd go out, drink, smoke and have long drunk lunches. His name was Eddie, and he's 'the second,' so he went by the 'Deuce.' Actually I never really wanted to go out. I was more or less over going to bars."

There was another factor contributing to his reluctance to go to nightclubs.

"Just before I left Atlanta, I read a little piece in *The Advocate* (a gay newspaper/magazine) about these two men in the Bay Area that had died of a strange illness that attacked their immune system, similar to Legionnaire's Disease. They were calling it G.R.I.D. then . . . gay related immune deficiency." Later, the acronym would be changed to A.I.D.S., for acquired immune deficiency syndrome.

"It was the big Biblical thing for me then, the hand coming out of the sky and saying, 'Get you back home, child, because you might die.' That was another reason I came back to Savannah. And I was basically celibate for several years. I had no contact with anyone, really, until I met Jesse in late 1988. Deuce and other friends kept trying to drag me to the bars, but usually I wouldn't go."

The celibacy ended with the introduction of Jesse Faucette III into his life.

"It was like, spontaneous combustion. Deuce introduced us, and this guy was just fascinated with me, and he was this gorgeous hunk of man. He was maybe six foot, two hundred and ten, muscles, blond hair, blue eyes . . . the beach boy from next door, the California surfer dude."

There was a complication to the attraction. Jesse was already involved with someone else.

"He was living with this other guy named John. Just before all the bad stuff in 1991 started happening, John made a trip to Buford, and I really believe he went there to do some kind of voodoo. Sort of a similar thing happens in *Midnight In The Garden of Good And Evil*. Larry (Smith) told me about that later. When he told me, I was in my period of just living to do crack, so I wasn't really too 'up' on anything mentally. I never thought about it until much later, when I was in the county jail."

The relationship between Martin and Faucette was initially a clandestine one. Jesse was still living with John. "Most of the time, he was slipping over to my house," Jim said.

The first disaster in the chain of horrors for Jim Martin in 1991 struck his friend, Deuce Jakes. In February, Jakes was badly hurt in an automobile accident.

"Somehow or other, they were doing some construction out on some of the interstate in the outlying areas of Savannah, out beyond Hunter Air Base," Martin explained. "They had moved a bunch of dirt, and Deuce swerved to avoid hitting a car and—I know this sounds fantastic, but this is how it was described to me and how I remember it—he went up this mound of dirt about 40 feet into the air. He had his seat belt on, and something about the belt and harness grabbed him and caused the blood flow to be stopped, so he ended up having a stroke because of the seat-belt thing over his neck. He was only thirty-two years old, and he was in ICU. I just literally went to pieces. This was my best friend."

It also brought forth another problem. With Deuce out of commission, Jim had lost his primary marijuana connection. He had been buying about two ounces per month, which he shared with Jesse when they were meeting. And by that time, they were meeting often and openly. Jesse had moved into his own apartment, "It was in a high rise, a Section 8 (government-assisted rental payments for low-income earners)."

About that time, Jim had also secured a job at Ben Portman's Music Center. "I did telemarketing. I worked on the phone and the computer, calling customers who'd bought band instruments and stuff like that."

Every day at lunchtime, he walked to Jesse's apartment, then back to work. At night, he walked from his home to Jesse's apartment and back. Shortly after Deuce's accident, either due to the excessive walking or due to kinky sexual aerobics, Jim developed a chronic pain in his hips and legs.

"I was taking quinine pills and my dad was giving me Indocin (a prescription drug), and none of it was doing any good. But I was still walking back and forth to his apartment.

"We hung out sometimes with some guys a couple of blocks from Jesse's apartment. I knew one of them from the loan company I'd worked at. He was the brother of one of our customers. Jesse knew him, too. There was a liquor store conveniently just a couple blocks away, and we'd go out on liquor runs."

At that apartment in 1990, Jim met Larry Smith, who sold marijuana to him and to Jesse and others who "hung out" there.

Jim had known of Larry Smith for some time. He had seen him in gay social circles in Savannah. A cross-dresser, Smith used the name "Latrice Boudair" when in female attire. Although Brenda

Kennedy, a Chatham County employee who was at the trial of Jim Martin, said that Smith, an African-American, had done impersonations of Diana Ross at local clubs, no one else would confirm that.

Until he and Jesse started "hanging out" at the friend's apartment, Jim had never been formally introduced to Smith. He described Smith as "slim and very affected. He always wore long colorful scarves and kind of flowing pants and caftan shirts and some make-up, but not real heavy drag. He wore lots of different colognes and perfumes. He was a tough, suspicious queen who also carried that giant knife. He was really pretty in a way, but vanity and cruelty and arrogance would be hard-pressed to stay hidden in his face."

One night in May of 1991, Martin found out that Smith was furnishing more than marijuana. What happened that night would cure the pain in his legs and hips, but it would lead to far greater pain in the long run.

"We'd be hanging out, and they would call Larry, and Larry would come over. Jesse and the brother (of the loan company customer) and Larry would go into the bathroom. The second time this happened, I got up on my high horse and stomped over there and said, 'What's going on?' One of them was sitting on the side of the tub, one on the toilet and they were passing this little pipe around. And Jesse said, 'Oh, go on and give him a hit.' I don't know how long this had been going on. Evidently, they had been smoking crack for a long time.

"And I'd swear this on a stack of Bibles: the moment I took a hit of that crack and felt the effect of it, all of my pain went away."

Crack cocaine has been said to be instantly addictive. Addicts, it has been reported, frequently say that the first time is the best, and that subsequent smoking is merely an attempt to duplicate the feeling of the first time.

"I've heard that over and over from the guys here in prison," Martin said. "But for me, every time I smoked it, I duplicated that first time."

And so he became an addict.

"I smoked every day from that day on. Hardly a day would go by when I didn't."

It was an expensive addiction.

"In the beginning, it was sometimes three hundred to four hundred dollars a day."

His sexual and social relationships continued with Jesse, but now he was also hanging out with Larry, too.

"I figured out after he gave me the first hit . . . and I felt like a million dollars suddenly . . . well, I'd say, 'Let's call him. I have some money.' Larry would pick me up, and we would go, and he would get it for me. I instantly became an addict."

There were some lines he did not cross.

"I never went to work (under the influence) on it. Even when I smoked pot, I never smoked on the job. I would go sometimes at lunch from the music store and meet Larry, and we'd go get some crack, and I'd hold onto it until that night and get together with Jesse.

"And I never crossed the line of having sex with Larry. He attempted to come on to me one time, but I wouldn't have any of that."

He said that Smith also never attempted to mix the trades of drugs and sex, which is reported to be common among crack users and dealers.

Even with the addition of the expensive addiction to Jim's life, things did not really begin to fall apart in the Martin household until Emerson Martin died in September.

"Up until that point, as far as I know, the relationship with my mother was just fine. He (Emerson) went in for open heart surgery in September. My mom and I were there, and we were all hugging each other. My dad was crying and saying, 'I don't want to leave you.' He knew he was going to die."

Before leaving home for the hospital, however, Emerson had had a calmer approach. "He came in and talked to us," Jim said. "He told us what to expect and how we were going to have to help him when he got home. And then he started having these little attacks, and I started falling apart. So did my aunt. But my mom, she was just calm, cool and collected. It was her higher power at work, she said."

Emerson had the surgery, but he died in the hospital shortly thereafter.

"They stabilized him after surgery, and the doctor told us that he would be going home in two weeks. They said everything was fine," Jim recalled. "But he started having attacks, whatever they were, and they started losing his heartbeat. They tried to resuscitate him, and they brought him back two times, but the third time they couldn't. My aunt and I were at his bedside. I saw his spirit leave through his mouth and his half-opened eyes . . . they were glittering . . . and I've felt it in me from that day to now."

Alva was also there.

"The afternoon we were at the hospital, Mom took me home. I wanted to go back and see Dad. I hadn't seen him since he left the house. Mom said, 'He's fine. Everything that can be done is being done for him,' but I insisted, and so we went back to the hospital about eight o'clock. Right after we got there was when they had to let him go."

Reactions from mother and son differed.

"My mother showed very little emotion at all," Jim said. "The only time I've ever seen her break down and cry was at the funeral home when her mother died, and her sister had told her, 'Alva, we can't cry over this.' And she turned it off then, just like a faucet.

"I'm very emotional, though. I take after my dad's family. We cry. We scream. I don't think I'll ever get over it (his death)."

Jim was also unhappy that he was not allowed to have input into the funeral service. "My mother would only allow me to pick out the casket," he said. "There were only two that would fit him, so I picked the cheaper one. I was not allowed to participate in planning the funeral, and this still rankles me years later. Neither did my dad's other children have any say-so in the funeral. One day, I would like to have a memorial service for him."

Barbara Perry maintains that Alva contributed to Emerson's death.

"He wasn't a happy person," she said. "He didn't enjoy the outside things because he couldn't do them. Until the last couple of years, he hid it. He was always a happy, jolly person. He was like a daddy to me, because he was so much older than me, and my daddy and I weren't close.

"I think (the stress of Alva's control) helped make his heart problems worse. And another thing, we told her time and time again, 'You're killing him with the food you're cooking.' My husband had the heart bypass operation in 1983, and they told us what not to eat and about cholesterol and that sort of thing. High cholesterol and heart attacks and strokes run in our family. Emerson weighed about 300 pounds. Alva was giving him gravy and roast beef and potatoes and rice. I told her, 'You'd better get him on a diet. It's going to kill him.' But she wouldn't stop. 'No, no, he's fine. He likes it. He likes his fried chicken. He can eat a whole fried chicken.' I told her over and over that it was killing him.

"She wouldn't listen. She didn't really want him to go to a doctor. The doctor she did go to was a quack. He did nothing about Emerson's heart condition. Emerson had a heart attack before Mother died, and Alva didn't even call us. Mother died in 1977, and it was several years before that. He was in the hospital. We only found out when somebody from the church called us and wanted to know how Emerson was.

"When he finally had his surgery . . . and I talked him into it, which is something I just have to live with . . . the doctor who did the surgery said his heart was as big as a football, just waiting to explode."

Perry also said there were cracks in the foundation of the relationship between Jim and Alva long before the crack cocaine and Emerson's death.

"Emerson would get fed up. Time and time

again, he'd come to our house and say, 'They're at it again. Sooner or later, one's going to kill the other.' This was probably two years before Emerson died. That was their little family thing, and they just didn't talk about it. But Emerson, about two years before he died, started talking about different things. Emerson was streetwise enough that he had to know that Jimmy was gay, but he didn't want to believe that, so I never talked with him about it. Alva was too naïve to realize that Jimmy was gay. When we talked to her the last time we saw her, she still didn't believe it."

Jim claims the brother-and-sister discussions between his father and his aunt were interpreted in an out-of-perspective way. "We were more or less content then," he said. Of course, given his deep-seated resentment for Alva, "content" may well be a relative (no pun intended) term. And other comments by Barbara Perry note that, at least after Emerson's death, mother and son were continually at odds.

Ralph Allen, Jim's boss at Ben Portman's Music Center, testified at the trial that he frequently overheard Jim in heated arguments with Alva on the telephone, and that he had heard Jim make threats. Jim claims that Allen was trying to discredit him as much as possible because Allen knew that it would come out in cross-examination that Allen had made sexual overtures to him. In his testimony, Allen categorically denied that he had done so. The allegation was rather unusual in that Martin claimed that both he and Allen had remained fully clothed during their sole physical encounter. . . and that there was nothing more than a simulation of sexual positions. Jim also claimed that Allen had hinted that he, not Jesse, would be a more suitable partner for him. Allen denied that he had ever had such a conversation.

After Emerson Martin died, Jim Martin's money ran out. He had quit his job at Ben Portman's Music Center. Driven by his crack cocaine addiction, he turned to two avenues to raise money to support the habit: selling possessions and stealing. The victim of his theft was his mother.

He forged checks from an account over which his mother had custody. Ultimately, Alva cashed in a savings' certificate and replenished those funds when she found out that her son had stolen the money.

After his father died, Jim began a run of credit card fraud. The first date documented by court proceedings was October 11. He bought at least two leather coats and two rope-chain necklaces with credit cards stolen from his mother.

"There was a tremendous amount charged to the credit cards," Barbara Perry said, suggesting that the receipts shown at the trial represented only a small percentage of the misuses. "He bought things for Jesse. He bought things for Larry. He bought more for Larry, I think. Emerson told me Jim bought gifts for both of them, even though Jesse was mean to Jim. One time he beat him up and broke his glasses."

(The beatings were referenced in court by the fact that Jim sometimes wore make-up to work to hide scars resulting from sadomasochistic sexual encounters.)

The forging of the checks and the start of the

credit card fraud got Jim Martin arrested. He was placed on probation. By that time, he was so wound up on the crack that "probation" was merely a word.

On November 21, a little less than three weeks before Alva Martin was murdered, Officer Terrell Jacobs personally served Jim with a petition to revoke his probation. The revocation hearing was scheduled to take place on January 6, 1992, more than two weeks after Jim was arrested for Alva's murder. One of the chief witnesses against Jim would have been his mother.

Meanwhile, Jim began selling possessions. At first, he sold only his own things, such as books, a valuable record collection and various electronics, including stereo equipment and two video cassette recorders. He sold a piano that had been given to him by his parents.

At the trial, Larry Smith readily admitted that he had helped Jim load and take furniture and other possessions to shops that bought such items. By December 10, the day of Alva's murder, Jim had more or less run out of things of his own to sell.

Barbara Perry said she was not in any way surprised at the news that Alva had been murdered.

"She (Alva) came up here and she had told me that she was having trouble with Jimmy then. I asked her how she and Jimmy were doing, and she said, 'Not very well.' I asked her what was going on, and she said, 'Jimmy made me promise I wouldn't talk about him.'"

With further persuasion, however, Alva confessed to her sister-in-law just how serious the situation was. "She said, 'Well, he tried to choke me.' I asked how, and she said, 'Well, he put a scarf around my neck.' That was what she said. I can't tell you the exact date, but it was sometime between September and November that he had done this."

According to court documents, the date of the discussion between Perry and Alva was October 15. That event was never brought up during Martin's murder trial. A *Motion In Limine* (See Appendix G for full details of the motion) was filed by the Defense before the trial to squelch any possibility that Perry would testify that Alva had told her of the choking incident. The motion also requested that the State refrain from using some other information.

"She didn't say how she got away from him (in the aborted choking attempt)," Perry said. "He wanted money or something, and they probably got into an argument. She didn't have any money at that time, but they argued all the time. They never could get along with each other, and he had gotten very hostile and mean toward her. Some of the neighbors had said they saw the two of them run out of the back door, and he was hitting her. Why they didn't call the police then, I don't know. As to the choking incident, she didn't say how she stopped him, or if he just stopped it, or what."

Martin denies ever trying to choke his mother, or even hitting her.

"Never!" he said adamantly. Although he did concede that his mind was frequently warped while he was smoking crack cocaine, he said, "I don't remember ever trying to choke her."

At any rate, the floodgates of the problems between mother and son had been opened wide at that point.

"Several times she had called us," Perry said.

"I don't remember the exact date, but she had called and asked if I would come down and talk to Jimmy, that she was having so much trouble with him taking things out of the house and selling them. So Robert and I went down there and talked to Jim.

"One time when I went, he didn't stay home very long. His friend, Larry, and several other boys met him, so we didn't get to talk much. But about a week or so before Alva died, she called me again and said Jimmy was getting ready to take the television out of the house and sell it, and would I please come down."

It was a Sunday morning when Alva called. After Barbara arrived, Alva wanted to leave for church. Barbara persuaded her to stay home.

"She stayed, and Jimmy and I went out in the yard and talked for about four hours. She had wanted me to talk to him into going and having counseling . . . going to like a mental health facility.

"We sat out in the yard for about four hours, and he talked to me about different things and the problems they were having. I finally talked him into going for treatment, but he told me, 'I want her to go with me.' So we went back into the house, and I told Alva that Jimmy had agreed to go to Charter if you go with him for the sessions."

Alva flatly refused.

"No, I won't go," Perry recalled Alva saying. "I don't need counseling. Jesus is my counselor, and I don't need counseling."

Jim's response to Alva's refusal: "Then I'm not going either."

The October choking incident never got much attention in the conversation between nephew and aunt.

"I mentioned it to him, but he never really commented on it," Barbara said.

When Barbara Perry and her husband left Savannah for their rural Georgia home that day, it seemed a foregone conclusion that Alva's death was imminent.

"Robert and I went and got into our car to go back home, and I said, just as soon as we walked outside, 'She sealed her death warrant today.' I knew she had."

December 10, 1991, was a Tuesday. The *Savannah Morning News* archive listed the weather for that day as sunny, with a high of 73 degrees and a low of 58. "It was clear," Jim recalled. "I think Larry and I ran around and got some money together and bought some crack earlier in the day."

According to Jim's testimony at his trial, Larry called him and said that he wanted to talk to Alva . . . that he and Jim needed to start making restitution to Alva for the misuse of her credit cards.

"He came over again that night," Jim said in an interview many years later. "He wanted to get some more crack. I don't really know what was on his mind. He was smoking along with me, maybe not as much as I was doing, though. So it's kind of hard to remember exactly how we thought back then. It was about seven or eight when he arrived."

Jim says he told Larry that he would go into the house and would try to find something to sell. Larry, he said, wanted to come along. They left Jim's trailer and entered the house through the back door.

"My mother was in the living room, sitting in

a chair, watching TV," Jim recalled, his last memory of seeing his mother alive. "She was probably watching *Jeopardy*. She liked that show, and it was about that time of the night. I went back to my room . . . an old room in the house that used to be mine. I still had some stuff there, mostly clothes and stuff."

He maintains that when he returned, minutes later, Alva was dead. He said he'd heard nothing.

"When I came back, he (Larry) had choked her. She was sitting in the chair, and her head was down, and he had something behind her neck, and there was blood kind of out of the corner of her mouth. I grabbed for the phone, but Larry knocked me and the phone to the ground. He was standing over me, he put his knee on my chest, and he had this knife.

"I'd seen the knife before. It's about this long (gesturing with hands about twelve inches apart), a good length, and you just kind of flick it and it extends. I don't know what you call it. He put that to my throat and he said, 'Look, you do what I tell you to do from here on out, or I'll kill you, too, and then I'll burn this house down and nobody will ever know what happened to you or your mother, either one of you.'"

One thing about that night that remains at least partially unexplained is the fact that Alva was beaten severely in the face before being strangled. Coroner Kris Sperry testified at the trial that the bruising was substantial, and that the beating had happened while she was still alive.

Jim says he has no recollection of seeing bruises. He says he heard nothing while he was in the room that would indicate any kind of struggle between Larry and Alva.

"She knew him," Jim said. "He talked to her when he came over there. She'd never said anything out of the way about him. She did have racial prejudices, but she was the type of person who was civil about it. More than my dad, for example."

Alva's death certificate showed her weight to be 149 pounds. Larry Smith weighed between 125 and 130. Jim says at the time he was approximately 140 pounds. It seems unlikely that either of them could have administered the brutal beating that the coroner's report indicated took place and killed Alva single-handedly.

Barbara Perry's theory is that her nephew did the killing and the beating that resulted in the bruising. But she doesn't think he was acting alone.

"I think Jim did the actual killing," she said. "I think he's responsible for the bruises they found on her face, too. She might have outweighed him, but he was a lot younger than she was, and he could have overpowered her. She was not very strong. She was a woman that did no physical labor whatsoever. She was the literary type that read and studied all the time. Plus she was in her seventies. If Jimmy had wanted to beat her up, he could have. But somebody had to help him tie her up and drag her and put her in the closet and hang the blanket over her. I don't think he could have done that by himself. So I feel that Larry and the other boy (Jesse) were involved. I feel there was help there. But I do feel that he (Jim) killed her, most likely in a fit of rage.

"I think it was a spur-of-the-moment thing. I don't think he planned it ahead. What I think happened is that he went in and asked her for money, and, being the way she was, she probably chewed him out, and a fight started, and he just grabbed her and choked her.

"I think Larry helped afterwards with the body. And I think Jesse was involved, too. He was involved in selling the stuff (items sold to get money for drugs). He benefited from what Jimmy was selling. I think they must have made a deal; I always thought they plea-bargained, which is why they never got any time."

Jesse Faucette was never called to testify at the trial, although his name was on the witness list for both the Prosecution and Defense. Bill Dowell, Defense Attorney at Jim Martin's trial, said he did not recall exactly why Jesse wasn't called to testify. Given that Dowell has been a part of a hundreds of cases and that roughly ten years had passed when he was asked the question, the reply did not come as a great surprise.

"I don't remember too much about that part," Dowell said. "It seems to me Jesse seemed very uninterested in any of it. I believe he told me he didn't recall at all how he had first met Larry Smith."

"I think the other boys helped wrap Alva up and put her in the closet, but I think Jimmy did it in a fit of anger. You can become so angry that sometimes you don't realize just what you're doing. I know. I have a terrible temper," Perry said. "I really think that Jim just went into a rage, and I'm sure she pushed him into it. There were times I wanted to choke her myself, and I'm sure Bettie (Emerson's daughter) felt like choking her a lot of times. I would never have choked Alva, but she did make me angry many times."

While Barbara Perry was not surprised that her nephew choked her sister-in-law, she does not regard it as "justifiable homicide."

"I think he should have walked away," she said, "but it doesn't make me love Jimmy any less. And I think I can understand why he did it. I don't accept it, but I understand why."

Although Barbara Perry terms Larry Smith as "dangerous," Jim says he never felt threatened until after his mother was dead.

"I'd never seen him fight. He'd talk about things he had done, but I'm not sure how much of it was just talk," Jim said. But never did Jim incur Larry's wrath, either. "I always paid up front, so there was never a situation where he would get mad at me. If I didn't pay, I didn't ride (to get the drugs)."

After the killing, the body of Alva Martin was wrapped up and hidden in a closet. Jim says that was Larry's idea.

"I think I was crying, but I was too shocked to react much," Jim said. "I just felt hopeless, like suddenly there was no future. I wondered what was going to happen to me."

What would happen was that Jim Martin and Larry Smith would continue to sell items from the Martin household, including the television that Alva had been watching when she was killed. Meanwhile, Jim told stories, to neighbors and to anyone else who would inquire, that Alva was alive and playing nursemaid at the home of a friend with a broken hip. He says Larry Smith forced him to create the illusion that Alva Martin was still alive.

"Right after he killed her, he said he was going to keep coming over, and we were going to keep selling stuff," Jim said. "We were going to try to sell the house. We were going to try to sell the car. He had all these schemes that we were going to use to make money."

So Larry's plan was to just leave the body in the closet and pretend it never happened?

"Yeah," Jim said. He sighed deeply at the thought, which, he said, triggered memories of missed opportunities to change the sequence of events. "The thing that hurt me so bad then . . . and now, too . . . is that when he left me alone I didn't immediately call the police. I never did call them."

He did not have to call them; the police came to him. Officer Donald Thompson came to the Martin household a few days before the body was discovered to check on the well-being of Alva Martin. Neighbors had notified the police that Alva's car, which she routinely drove daily for her errands, had not been moved in several days, and that Alva herself had not been seen. Jim not only did not tell Thompson that Alva was dead; he told the officer the same story he was giving everyone else: his mother was attending to a woman with a broken bone, and that his mother was being picked up and driven to see the lady that she was helping.

In court, he testified that he would have liked to have told Officer Thompson what had happened, but that Larry had called shortly before the officer had arrived, and he was afraid. Because of fear and because of his passive personality, he said he was completely under Larry's control.

When asked what it was like to continue to associate with the man that he claimed had killed his mother, Jim Martin replied, "I really don't remember much about it. Larry would come over every day and take me around, and we sold stuff. I was in shock. I was terrified. I was scared. There are some things in life that you don't have a script for. This was one of them. I didn't know what to do. I was a big, fat crybaby."

His crybabyism notwithstanding, Jim made efforts to keep anyone from knowing his mother was dead.

"Larry told me I had to get on the phone and impersonate her voice so people wouldn't wonder," Jim said. "He made me make up this story that she was taking care of somebody. I never knew why he didn't try to get rid of her body. Maybe he was planning all along to set me up for it . . . to get the last dollars and then get me out of his hair."

Owen Ferguson said that it was Jim's phone impersonations of Alva Martin that reminded him of the horror movie *Psycho*. "You see the person in the chair, and you think it's a woman, but it turns out to be a man. That's why this case always reminds me of the Bates Motel."

Jim said that Larry had also threatened to kill Jesse if he relayed the story to his partner. "I don't remember how much I saw Jesse then (after the killing). I think might have seen him one time. I don't remember if we had sex."

Jim called neighbors, who testified in court that they weren't fooled by his attempts to impersonate his mother's voice. He called Goodwill Industries, where Alva held a weekly worship service, to give regrets that she would be unable to attend.

He also called at least one creditor, pretending to be his mother, asking that charges against him be dropped. All these things, he claims, were scripted by Larry Smith. Smith testified in court that he had once spoken on the phone for several minutes with someone he thought was Alva Martin, but it had turned out to be Jim doing an impersonation. Smith testified he had been "somewhat shocked."

Denise Overland, a secretary at Goodwill Industries, said she received a phone call on December 12, and that a person who identified "themselves as Reverend Alva Martin" was sick with the flu and could not come to hold chapel service. Overland said, "The voice sounded like a younger female."

The stories of Jim's impersonations of Alva and the story of the friend with the broken hip (or leg) were repeated by several different witnesses in court. Barbara Perry was also told the same story. She recalls talking to Jim "numerous times" between December 10 and the discovery of the body.

"I'd say, 'Hey, Jim, how's Alva? Can I speak to your mama?' And he would say, 'Well, she's not here right now; she's over at Stillwell Towers.' And one time he told me she was going to spend the night over there and help someone named Anita, and that didn't sound right. Alva wouldn't have done that. She'd have gone and had a worship service and washed her hands and left. That didn't fit."

Jim said that he spent as little time in the

house as possible while his mother's body was in the closet. "I was doing the same things I'd been doing, but I still did them in the trailer. I didn't go in the house very much. I tried to stay out of there."

"He did go in, though," Barbara Perry said. "There were dirty dishes in there, and evidence of where he had fed his cats and things like that, and where he had bathed. So he was in and out of the house."

Finally, on the night of December 19, Sergeant Ted Workman was making yet another follow-up call to determine the well-being of Reverend Martin. Her absences from her regular duties as a pastor, compounded by her absence noted by her neighbors, had become ever more conspicuous. Workman was joined a few minutes later by Detective Linda Hansen.

After checking the house and finding it locked, Workman testified at the trial that he was attempting to gain entry to the house via the back door when he was hit by an odor coming from inside the house.

"Through my twenty-five . . . years of police experience, I determined that odor to be death," he testified.

Before he could gain entry to the house, Jim Martin came to meet the officers. Workman testified that initially Martin refused to let them into the house, but when told that the police would go in "with or without a key," Martin produced a key and unlocked the back door.

While Jim Martin sat in the living room, perhaps in the same chair in which Alva Martin had sat while being strangled, officers searched the house. According to Workman's court testimony, Jim "watched where we were going. He stood up several times when I got close to the closet." Workman discovered the body in a clothes closet. He said that several deodorizers were hanging in the closet.

Workman testified that when he found the body, at first "I found two white socks, sticking up in the air, at which point I felt one of the socks, and I could feel something in it."

The "something" was Alva Martin's foot.

Jim Martin was placed in handcuffs and advised that he was under arrest.

After the Arrest

It was after midnight in Savannah, 12:10 a.m. according to police notes, when Jim Martin was brought to the Chatham County Police Department. He was turned over to Detective Owen Ferguson. They were left alone in a room approximately twelve feet square.

At that point, Jim Martin testified at his trial, he was relieved to have found someone to talk to. He still confirms that relief. He made a short statement to Ferguson.

"I had never been so glad to see anyone as I was him," Martin said in an interview years later. "I thought he was coming to my rescue and going to make everything okay. I cried from grief and relief. But after a few minutes of that, he shut me up by saying, 'You're crying because you got caught.' From then on, the whole case was told from his spin, and every word that came out of his mouth was the gospel."

Ferguson retired from the police force in 2003. He said that he had worked "a couple hundred" homicides during his career. He reviewed his notes from his encounter with Martin and recalled, "Nowhere do I remember or did I document that he was relieved. He showed no emotions or sympathetic thoughts. Realistically, he could have been relieved, but he didn't say it to me.

"He wasn't really a hard individual to deal with, though. He just sucked it up and went on with it."

Ferguson's testimony at the trial also gives no indication that the accused was relieved or in any way happy to see him. In a preliminary hearing regarding the timing of the reading of Miranda rights and the validity of the statement that Martin made (and signed), Ferguson summed up the statement he was given:

"I asked him straight out why he killed his mother. And with that, he just looked at me with a sly remark and says, in a laughing manner, 'Why, I didn't do that.' And, admittedly, it sort of went in the wrong way when he said it. He just laughingly said, 'I didn't do that.' And he said, 'Well, Larry did it.' And he smiled at me, and I said, 'Well, then, tell me about Larry.'

"And he commenced to tell me about a black male that had come over to his house on December 10, 1991, by the name of Larry Smith, and he said that he had strangled her to death with a . . . with a tie. Larry made him wrap her up in a blanket and tie her up like a pig and hide her in the closet, which he did."

Until then, Ferguson said, Martin had made no request for a lawyer. "When I had a tape recorder to tape the conversation, as we normally do, he stated he wanted his lawyer. At that point, the interview was terminated. After that, he wanted another cigarette, but he was locked in a cell and told he was charged by murder."

Martin said that he had had two beers and that he had also smoked crack cocaine just before the police arrived at the house. Although he testified that he was still "under the influence of the drugs at the time" that he made and signed his statement, District Attorney Ron Adams brought up the point that two beers and crack cocaine smoked at 10 p.m. would have lost most of the effect by the time of the interview with Detective Ferguson. The point was raised during a hearing before the trial regarding the admissibility of the statement that Martin had signed in the presence of Ferguson.

The Defense had sought to block the statement on the grounds that Martin had been under the influence of drugs and alcohol at the time that his rights had been read to him, and that he had not fully understood what he was doing when he had made and signed the statement. The Prosecution contended that he was fully aware of what he had been doing.

"Mr. Martin knew what I was talking about. He questioned me about the waiver and signed it. In no way, shape or form was there anything wrong with his understanding at that time, in my opinion," Ferguson said in the hearing.

At the conclusion of the hearing, Judge Perry Brannen Jr. ruled that the statement could be used as evidence during the trial.

Barbara Perry was summoned to the police station later in the day. "I hadn't been there too long before they told me I had a telephone call, and it was Jim. As soon as I answered the phone, he said, 'Barbara, I did it.' Then he said, immediately after, 'Larry made me do it.' And immediately after that, he said, 'Larry did it.' Those were his first comments to me."

In court, she had testified to the same thing, only the wording was, "Barbara, I killed her." Those words would show up in the headlines of the *Savannah Evening Press* on the day of her testimony.

From that point on, Jim Martin attended to whatever details to which he could attend from the jail cell. He wrote to Jesse and got no response. His aunt came to visit regularly. She agreed to care for his cats, Cotton and Miss Kitty.

"They're gone now," Barbara Perry said. "They stayed with us for several years. They'd never been outside till they'd been here, and I let them go out and play. Jim got upset about that at first, but after he realized they were enjoying themselves, he was okay."

The cats had been Jim Martin's companions for several years. The fact that they were among his top concerns in letters he wrote from prison to Barbara Perry was brought to light during questioning at the trial.

"You cared enough about your cats to recount the things that you and your cats had done for several years, did you not?" District Attorney Ron Adams asked Martin in cross-examination. Upon receiving an affirmative response, he followed with, "But you didn't care enough about your mother to even recognize or mention that she was dead." Although Jim replied, "That's not true at all," Adams had made his point to the jury that, at least in terms of his correspondence with his aunt, the cats were Jim's priority.

"Yes, I wrote to my aunt about the cats," Martin said later. "I was concerned about them. They were alive. They needed care. They were my babies. We had lived together for about eleven years in that small trailer. They had been very sheltered, and now they had been taken out of the trailer by strangers and spent the night in an animal shelter."

The Trial

On February 2, 1993, at 10:18 a.m., more than a year after Alva Martin's murder, the proceedings began for the trial of her son, accused of her killing. The trial was Case No. CF92-0747-B, Murder (1), Felony Murder (1), State of Georgia vs. James Mize Martin. Chatham County Superior Court Judge Perry Brannen Jr. presided over the case.

After questioning potential jurors through questions and answers that covered one hundred pages of transcripts, an all-female jury was empanelled by 1:49 p.m. Three prospective jurors were disqualified on the basis of pre-trial opinion. Patrick Henry Merritt was disqualified when he said he knew the defendant. Another prospect, identified only as Mrs. Webb, claimed to have known the Martin family. Another remarked that his parents lived next door to Bloomingdale Church of the Nazarene, where Alva Martin had served as minister.

At the time of jury selection, Jim Martin was optimistic. An all-female jury, he felt, would be more sympathetic to his plight. Later, he changed his mind, citing that he and his defense attorney should have realized that women would not necessarily be the most sympathetic jurors to a man who had allegedly killed his mother. Nor, he reckoned, would they be any more tolerant of his homosexuality.

Defense Attorney Bill Dowell was forty-six years old when the case went to trial. He had worked in the District Attorney's office from 1976 through 1981 before "switching sides." He said he typically handled four to eight murder cases per year, but many of them were "pled down to voluntary manslaughter."

After the jury was chosen and the court had recessed for an hour for lunch, the jury was removed for a hearing, called "Jackson Denno Hearing," to resolve any possible impropriety in the reading of Miranda rights to the defendant. Owen Ferguson, to whom Martin was turned over when he was taken into custody, claimed Martin signed a waiver of his rights. Martin claimed that he had not understood what he was doing. "I'd had approximately two beers to drink and smoked some crack cocaine . . . very shortly before the police arrived at my house," he testified.

Ferguson testified, "He may have been under the influence, but I couldn't tell you what (drugs or alcohol) they were. But Mr. Martin knew what I was talking about. He questioned me about the waiver before he signed it."

Prosecuting Attorney Ron Adams, when questioning Martin for the state, educed Martin to testify to the timing of his alcohol and drugs, which, for all intents and purposes, doomed any hopes the defense might have had of having the statement invalidated.

Martin testified that he had had the two beers

two to three hours before his interview with Ferguson. The crack cocaine had preceded the interview by at least ninety minutes, according to Martin's testimony.

"Crack cocaine is a very quick-acting drug, is it not?" Adams asked.

"Yes, it is," Martin replied.

"And it is also very quick in losing the effects of it once you've done it, is that not correct?"

"Somewhat."

Adams then hit the bull's-eye. "In fact, it's not unusual to smoke crack cocaine and then an hour later take another hit of it?"

Martin agreed, and his "under the influence" contention about his condition at the time he had signed the waiver of rights was dead. The jury returned at 3:30 p.m. and was duly sworn in.

Adams' opening statement was comprehensive, outlining the state's case. The highlights of the opening argument included:

— That the accused had, with malice aforethought, killed Alva Martin via strangulation with a bandanna.

— That the accused and the victim had had a rapidly deteriorating relationship in the time prior to the night of the victim's death.

— That the Defendant had misused his mother's credit cards, that he had had indicated on more than one occasion that he did not like what his mother stood for, and that he had stated on "more than two occasions" that he could kill his mother.

— That the body had been kept for many days after death, and the Defendant made a "conscious effort . . . to perpetuate the fraud that his mother was . . . still alive."

— That the Defendant, during the time he was fraudulently maintaining that his mother was alive, took pieces of furniture out of his mother's house to sell to pawn shops and to used furniture shops.

— That the Defendant, upon seeing his dead mother upon the discovery of her body, looked at her, made no comment of any kind, turned and walked away. He had "made no emotional response of any kind."

— That the Defendant claimed that Larry Smith was actually the killer, and that Larry Smith would be testifying during the trial as to his relationship with the Defendant.

— That the Defendant told his aunt that he had killed his mother, then recanted that statement and said, "No, I didn't do it, Larry did. Larry made me hide the body."

In summation, Adams concluded: "Now I expect . . . that the Defendant is going to come before you and tell you that he didn't have anything to do with this crime, that he was there and that it happened and that, while he did nothing to prevent it, he shouldn't be held accountable for it. I want you to listen to the evidence as it comes before you, and I want you to decide at the end of this trial whether or not the Defendant either committed this murder or was a party to this murder."

Dowell had a much shorter opening statement. "We expect the evidence to show that Larry Smith is a crack dealer and that he literally enslaved James Martin. We expect to show that, at this stage, he (Smith) is the one who should be on trial. . . . We're not going to paint a picture that James Martin is totally innocent. We're not going to deny that he was aware of the existence (of the body) as far as it being in the closet, but we would offer the explanation as to why he did it and why Larry Smith made him do it."

The first witness for the prosecution was Dr. Kris Sperry, forensic pathologist, contracted by the Georgia Bureau of Investigation. At the time he was employed by the Fulton County Medical Examiner's office in Atlanta. Sperry said he had performed 2,599 autopsies and made 179 previous court testimonies. He had a good reason to remember the autopsy of Alva Martin. It had occurred on December 21, Sperry's birthday. The autopsy, he said, had taken three hours to complete.

"My opinion," Sperry testified, "is that Mrs. Martin died as the consequences of a ligature strangulation, in conjunction with blunt force injuries or severe bruising of the face, the left shoulder and the arms."

It was clear, said Sperry, that Alva Martin was beaten before her death.

"Clearly the finding of the hemorrhage or the bleeding in the tissues, the bruising, indicates that these injuries occurred before she died. The extent of the beating on the face was very severe. . . . I found that the hemorrhage was very deep and went to the muscles around the cheekbones and the soft tissues beneath the cheekbones and was very extensive."

Sperry testified that, by his best estimate, Mrs. Martin had been dead between one and two weeks, making the December 10 date of death credible. Because a bandanna was found around her neck, and because the strangulation could have been caused by that bandanna, Sperry concluded that it was probably the murder weapon.

Martin has adamantly maintained that the scarf or bandanna found on his mother's neck was not what Smith used to kill his mother. He testified at the trial that Smith used a necktie that he took from Jim's bedroom, but he can't account for how or when Smith got the tie. At no time in his recollection of the night of the murder did he mention that Smith had been in his bedroom, although he did testify that Smith had come to his trailer.

Upon cross-examination from Dowell, Sperry testified that he thought the bandanna was already on Mrs. Martin "for decorative purposes and it was utilized (to kill her) because it was there. It wasn't necessarily placed around her neck specifically to strangle her."

Could the bruising have occurred just seconds after Mrs. Martin was killed?

"Not to the extent that she had (the bruising), especially involving her face and head. No." Sperry testified.

Mary Turner, a neighbor on Livingston Avenue who had known the family "from when little Jimmy was about four years old" was the next witness. She testified that she passed the Martin home several times daily and saw Alva Martin "every day." After two days of not seeing her neighbor, she had called the police.

"Did you make any attempts to contact Mrs. Martin herself?" Adams questioned.

"I called . . . and asked for Mrs. Martin, and Jimmy (answered and) said, 'This is she.' I said, 'No, this is not Mrs. Martin. Let me speak to your mother.' He waited a few minutes. He come back again, he said, 'This is Mrs. Martin. I'm sick. I've got a cold,' or something. I said, 'No way.'

"Then Jimmy called me up and said, 'I know you're lonesome and you live by yourself.' I said, 'I'm lonesome 'cause I just lost my husband, but I don't live by myself. My son and my son-in-law live with me.' And he said, 'You got some dogs?' I said, 'Yeah.' He said, 'Will it bite?' I said, 'Yes, they will.'"

Mary Turner testified that she continued to press to speak to Alva. "He (Jim) said that she was gone nursing somebody, and I said, 'Well, the car's in the yard.' He said, 'Well, somebody comes and gets her, and she's going to stay over there nursing them people until the lady gets well.' And I didn't believe that, either."

When questioned about Larry Smith, Mrs. Turner testified that she'd seen "a tall black male in a robe coming and going often," and that she had never seen the man talking to Alva. "Just to Jimmy."

Ralph Allen was the next witness called by Ron Adams. Allen had been Jim Martin's supervisor at Portman's Music Center, where Jim had worked from the spring of 1991 until September of 1991. His testimony was highly damning to his former employee.

Allen said he had frequently spoken with Mrs. Martin on the telephone when she called to speak to her son at work.

"Did you ever have occasion to hear the

defendant having conversation with his mother on the phone?" Adams asked.

"Yes, sir," Allen replied. "Jim would be very agitated with his mother on the phone and be upset with her. And the outbursts like that are what I recall. After several (agitated outbursts), I told Jim that we could not have conversation like that in a business and carry on . . . that it was just not proper to have those kind of outbursts. And still, that still didn't calm down the conversations that he had.

"Jim would scream at his mother . . . complain to his mother. And he would repeat things back to me that, you know, he did not like about it."

Did, Adams asked, Allen ever have occasion to discuss with Jim the relationship between mother and son?

"Yes, sir. In October . . . he got very agitated with his mother on the phone. There was a partition between my office and his, a glass partition that I could see around and also hear around. He turned around; he knew that I had heard and he knew that I was not pleased with it in a professional manner. And he told me he was going to kill his mother."

"What, if anything did you do?"

"I spoke with his father about the outbursts themselves, about what he had said about his mother, and, you know, spoke with Mr. Martin on several occasions about the outbursts. Jim's father brought Jim to work every day. In my knowing Mr. Martin, Jim's father, he was a very, very nice man, and he was very polite to me. I was concerned about what he (Jim) had said and I did speak to him (Emerson Martin) about it."

Cross-examination by Dowell suggested that Allen had interests in Jim Martin beyond employment.

"Did you ever have contact with Mr. Martin over at his trailer?" Dowell asked.

"When I took him home . . . on two occasions, I have, sir," Allen responded.

"Did you ever go in the trailer with him, and have him give you a foot massage?"

"I went in the trailer with him and saw his cats, and he showed me some pictures of things he had collected. You know, pictures of movie stars and things like that."

"Isn't it true that when you went to leave, Jim hugged you, and then you made some advances toward him?"

"Absolutely not!" Allen insisted.

"You didn't try to persuade him to leave his companion and start dating you?"

"Absolutely not, sir, no."

Delma Henley and her daughter and son-in-law, Sandra and Julius Maginley, were the next witnesses for the Prosecution. They lived in the house next door to Alva Martin on Livingston Avenue. Mrs. Henley was the first to testify. Her testimony was the last of the opening day's proceedings.

Mrs. Henley said she had known Alva Martin "off and on" for thirty years, although she had only moved in with her son-in-law about a year prior to Alva Martin's murder. She and Alva were obviously close friends, as Mrs. Martin had had her mail forwarded to Mrs. Henley after Emerson Martin's death. Since Alva was not making the daily journey to Mrs. Henley's to pick up mail, an immediate flag went up in her mind. The absence was even more conspicuous because of the fact that her car had not been moved.

"Jimmy called me (a few days) before (the police found) the b6dy. He simply said that the reason I hadn't seen his mother was because she had gone to a friend of hers that had broken her hip and was taking care of her."

"Did the Defendant represent being Jim Martin or someone else?" Adams asked.

"(He said he was) his mother. I just let him go and think that I thought it was his mother. But I talked to him that afternoon, and he told me about his mother then, again. He said he'd heard from his mother. He said she was still taking care of the lady that broke a hip."

Julius Maginley said he had lived next door to the Martins for more than thirty years. He recalled the days before Alva's body was discovered, noting that Mrs. Martin was a person of routine, which included picking up her mail daily from Delma Henley.

Dowell questioned Julius Maginley about Larry Smith. Dowell did not use Smith's name, but referred to him as a "tall, thin black male."

"I have seen him on certain occasions," Maginley said. He confirmed Dowell's allegation that the man in question drove a green station wagon, and he said that his suspicions had been so deep that he had called the police and given them the license number of the station wagon.

"Did you ever see them (the black male and Jim) moving furniture from the house?" Dowell asked.

"Yes, sir."

Maginley's wife, Sandra, was next to testify. She confirmed the regularity of the routine of Alva Martin. Adams asked if she recalled "anything that appeared unusual" beyond Alva's absence.

"Yes, sir," Sandra Maginley answered. 'We had not seen her, and then it seemed like all of a sudden everything was being moved out of her house, like they were moving out."

When asked about Jim's explanation of Alva's absence, she rephrased what her husband had said: "Jimmy had told my husband that his mother was sitting with an elderly lady in Stillwell Towers that had broke her hip. And then he had changed it to a numbered street, which we thought was awful funny. And her car had not moved, and when (Julius) asked Jimmy about the car, he said some friends of hers had come and picked her up and took her there."

"Did you see the Defendant on December 19?" Adams asked.

"Yes, sir. There was a lot of furniture out in the back yard, and there was a blue cab that came up. They loaded that cab up. Then a station wagon came. They loaded the station wagon up. Then another cab came up, and they loaded it with furniture."

There was also a console television set.

"It was a big TV. After the first taxicab that came, him and the taxi driver loaded it into the cab," Sandra Maginley said.

Officer Donald Thompson was next to testify. He had been sent to Alva Martin's home a few days before the discovery of the body to follow up on neighbors' questions about her absence. When asked if he had had contact with the Defendant, he pointed to Jim Martin, clad in a blue shirt and dark blue sweater.

"(I was dispatched to) his mother's residence on Livingston Avenue . . . to check on her welfare. About ten-thirty to eleven in the morning. As I arrived, I pulled into the driveway, and as I was getting out of the car, Mr. Martin came from behind the house and approached my vehicle."

"Did you indicate to Mr. Martin the reason for your being there?" Adams questioned.

"Yes. He asked me if he could help me. I asked if he lived there. He said, 'yes,' he did. I indicated I was there to check on his mother. He indicated that a friend of his mother's had broken her leg, and that she was visiting her and had been so for a few days. I asked about her car. I asked if the car in the driveway was hers, and if she was out town, why had she not taken her car with her? He indicated that somebody had come and taken her, instead of her using her own car."

Sergeant Ted Workman, the man who found Alva Martin's body, was next to testify.

"I was sent over there to check on the well being of the victim, and I was also advised that the son was at the residence. I was going to try to make contact with the son, to get some information.

"I arrived. Detective Hansen arrived a short while later, and Lieutenant Davis arrived (later still). I was the first one on the scene. It was a little after 10 p.m."

"What did you do when you first got there?"

Adams asked.

"I was advised that he (Jim Martin) was on the premises somewhere. Someone had called. The info I received over the radio was (that) he was around the residence and to make contact with him. I checked the residence. I couldn't locate him. I then, along with Detective Hansen, checked the house. I checked all the doors, I looked in the windows. We beat on the door and rang the doorbell several times. Both (front and rear) doors."

"When you were about the rear door, did you make any observations that you considered unusual or significant?"

"Yes, sir, but prior to that I noticed a small camper-type trailer at the back of the residence, and extension cords and power were running from the house to the trailer. I beat on the door of the trailer with no response at the time. I then went to the back door (of the house), which I later found entered into the kitchen. You could see through the panes of glass. There were no curtains or blinds obstructing the view. I couldn't see anything or anybody inside. The screen door was open. I was trying to 'jimmy' the lock to gain entry, at which time I smelled an odor coming from inside the house.

"Through my twenty-five . . . twenty-six years of police experience, I determined that to be the odor of death. At about this time, the Defendant came walking up from the area near the trailer. At this point, I didn't say anything about the odor. I asked him who he was. He could have been a neighbor or somebody. He said he lived there, told me his name. I explained to him that we were there inquiring about the welfare of his mother. He said his mother wasn't home. I asked him where she was or where I could contact her.

"He said his mother was at Stillwell Towers with a friend who had fallen and broken her hip. She'd been with this friend house-sitting or nursing her, for several days. I asked him for a phone number or some way to contact her. He couldn't supply a name. He said he didn't know a phone number. I then asked him if he had a key to the house. He initially denied us permission to go into the house. I told him we were going to enter the house with or without a key."

Jim Martin gave the officers the key at that point. Thompson, Hansen, Davis and Martin entered the house.

"The odor of death was much stronger inside. At this point, we started looking through the house. We had the Defendant sit on a couch or chair in the living room. Lieutenant Davis stayed with him. Detective Hansen and I started to look through the house, room-by-room, just trying to pinpoint the (cause of the odor). There was a small closet in the hallway near the bedrooms. Sort of like a clothing closet, a coat closet.

"Initially when I opened the door, there was a . . . sort of rollaway bed that was pushed up to the door. There was clothes hanging from hangers across the bar over the top of the bed. Jackets and clothes. That's the only thing I could see initially in the closet. I (moved) the clothes to one side, at which point I found that between the bed and the back of the closet were several bags of what appeared to be Christmas presents, Christmas wrapping. There was a clothes basket of what appeared to be dirty clothes, and several items stacked up between the bed and the rear of the closet.

"As I was moving some of the stuff from on top of this stuff, just moving it out the way, I found two socks, two white socks, sticking up in the air, at which point I felt one of the socks, and I could feel something in it."

When he removed the sock, Workman said he found a partially decomposed foot.

"At that time I went back out to where the Defendant was sitting, advised him that he was under arrest. We placed him in cuffs, notified detectives and the ID people and did not disturb what was apparently a crime scene."

What, Adams asked, was the Defendant's reaction to the searching and subsequent arrest?

"He watched where we were going. He stood up several times when I got close to the closet, but he never did come down to where I was. (It was) very unusual. He made no comments, asked no questions, showed no emotions. He didn't ask anything. (After the arrest), he was cuffed and sat back on the couch or chair or whatever he was sitting on. I went and telephoned the police department and had them notify the proper people to come out and called for a unit to transport him (Martin) to the police department."

Detective Linda Hansen, next to testify, recalled Martin's mood before entering the house. Initially, she said, when the detectives started entering the back door, Jim had turned to walk away.

"I asked him, 'Where are you going?' And he

said that this was spooky, that we were scaring him. And I said, 'You need to come inside with us to check on your mother.'"

The following afternoon, Detective Hansen interviewed Robert and Barbara Perry.

"Did you conduct an interview with the aunt and uncle of the Defendant?" Adams questioned.

"Yes, on Friday, December 20, about 1:30 in the afternoon. During the interview there was a telephone call from Mr. Martin . . . to Mrs. Perry."

"Did Mrs. Perry answer the phone and talk on it?"

"Yes, she did."

Susan Phail and Denise Overland, the State's next two witnesses, were employed by Goodwill Industries. Alva Martin had been chaplain there and held chapel services every Thursday. Ms. Phail said she had received a phone call from someone who claimed to be "Sister Alva Martin."

"She was sending her regrets that she couldn't do the service for the Christmas party, which was to be on Friday. It sounded like her. I cannot be certain if it was her or her son."

Denise Overland also received a call. "A call was switched over to my desk, and a person identifying themselves as Reverend Martin stated that she would not be able to come that morning to conduct the chapel service, which is usually held at eleven o'clock, because she was sick with the flu.

"The voice sounded like a younger female."

Freddie Blige and Shelton Mitchell, drivers for Adams Cab, testified for the State. Blige said he had hauled a load of furniture in the trunk of his cab on the afternoon of December 19. "Some miscellaneous tables and so forth to the best of my remembrance. I took him to one of those antique type stores and . . . whatever transaction he did, he did it. He paid me and I left."

Mitchell said he arrived at the Martin residence about four p.m. on Dec. 19. He found Jim Martin waiting for him.

"He had a console TV and he told me he wanted to take it . . . to American Pawn Shop."

Nobody else accompanied Martin to the pawn shop, Mitchell said, but later he had Martin as a fare once again.

"I was dispatched to the Kroger's at Gwinnett and Habersham and took him to Livingston Avenue, the same place I had picked him up earlier in the day."

Martin charged items and pawned them for cash and also bought Smith expensive gifts as part of the compensation for his services as a drug agent. That led to Martin stealing and using his mother's credit cards. Lance Parker and Shannon Hammond, who worked for Belk's at Savannah Mall, testified.

Parker, Security Manager for Belk's, confirmed four purchases of jewelry, the first from Oglethorpe Mall for "fine jewelry," and the others from Savannah Mall, all rope chains. After a call from Mrs. Martin, he "ordered a pull on the credit card."

The four purchases totaled just over $2,200.00.

Shannon Hammond, a store detective, had spoken to Alva Martin to inform her that the account was being closed. Later, Hammond received another call.

"Between the first of December and Thanksgiving I received a telephone call in my office."

"Who did the caller identify themselves as?" Adams asked.

"Reverend Alva Martin."

"Were you able to determine at that point whether it was or was not the Reverend Martin?"

"It was not. The person on the phone stated they would like to drop everything against James Martin."

"Could you tell the gender of the person who was making this call?"

"No, I could not."

Sandra Brown and Doug Chartrand, from American Used Furniture, both testified that they had had contact with Jim Martin. Brown said she had bought a couple of pieces of furniture. Chartrand said he had had contact with Martin "just before Christmas," possibly on December 19. "He mentioned something about a piano, and I told him we didn't purchase pianos."

Terrell Jacobs, Martin's Probation Officer, added to the State's evidence.

"Mr. Jacobs, I hand you what has been marked States' Exhibit 33 and ask if you can identify that exhibit," Adams said.

"This is a petition for revocation. It alleged that he has violated the conditions of probation as such, condition number one, violate the criminal laws of any government authority, as stated, offense of credit card fraud, and has failed to pay on his fines and fees and restitution.

"The Defendant was served personally, one

on one, on the twenty-first of November, 1991."

Among the witnesses listed on that petition, a copy of which was given to Jim Martin, was Alva Martin. The revocation hearing was scheduled for January 6, 1992.

Next to testify was Larry Smith. Brenda Kennedy, who was working as a court official, recalled Smith's testimony as the thing she remembered most about the trial.

"He was elegant," Kennedy said of Smith. "He seemed so intelligent. When I heard him testify, I said to myself there was no way he (Larry) killed anyone, that the boy had killed his own mama."

Kennedy's other distinct memory from the trial was when Workman testified about the discovery of the body. "It was those (deodorizers) hang-ups in the closet, trying to cover up the death smell. That's the one thing I remember above everything else except for Larry."

Because his role in the melodrama of Alva Martin's murder is so significant, Smith's testimony is being presented in full:

Adams: How long have you known Mr. Martin, please, sir?

Smith: About two years

Adams: When did you first make acquaintance with Mr. Martin?

Smith: It was in the summer of 1990, I think.

Adams: All right. Would you describe your relationship with the defendant?

Smith: We were social acquaintances. I met him through another friend of mine.

Adams: All right, sir. Have you had the

occasion to be at the residence of the Defendant?

Smith: I have gone to his house, yes. He lived in a trailer in the back of the residence.

Adams: How many times have you been to that residence?

Smith: Oh, a dozen or more.

Adams: Now, do you know who lived in the home or the house there at that location?

Smith: His mother and father.

Adams: And do you recall that at some point in time that his father, Mr. Emerson Martin, died?

Smith: Yes, I do.

Adams: And would you still have an occasion to be in company with the Defendant during that period of time?

Smith: Yes, I was.

Adams: Have you ever had an occasion to be inside the home of Mr. and Mrs. Martin?

Smith: I was occasionally inside of the home, yes.

Adams: Have you ever had the occasion to telephone the Defendant at home?

Smith: Yes.

Adams: Have you ever had an occasion to telephone the Defendant when he would answer the phone and indicate he was someone other than himself?

Smith: Yes.

Adams: Would you describe that to the jury, please?

Smith: Well, I would call him up sometimes because I gave him rides where he needed to go. Usually his mother would answer, and I would say, "Good evening, Mrs. Martin. May I speak to Jim, please? How are you today?" And she usually would say, "Fine. Let me see where Jim is." And it took a couple of minutes for her to go and get him. I called once and he answered the phone, and I thought it was his mother because it sounded a lot like her, so I said what I always say: "Good evening, Mrs. Martin. How are you today? May I speak to Jim?" And we carried on a conversation for about five or six minutes, and then suddenly he laughed and said, "I got you, didn't I?" And I was somewhat shocked because I thought I actually was talking to Mrs. Martin.

Adams: During the time you were having contact with the Defendant, did the Defendant ever purchase for you any items of personal property?

Smith: Yes, he did. He purchased two leather coats, I think, and a silver necklace and bracelet.

Adams: Now, the leather coats . . . do you know where they were purchased?

Smith: At the Merry Go Round at Oglethorpe Mall.

Adams: And were you present when they were purchased?

Smith: I was present, yes.

Adams: All right. Do you know how the purchase was accomplished?

Smith: I think he paid for them with a credit card.

Adams: Do you know who that credit card was issued to?

Smith: I can't say that I exactly knew who it was issued to, and even though I was standing next to him when he signed, I wasn't really paying attention to whose name was on the card. So I can't really say that I saw a name on the card. As far as I was concerned, they were his. That's what he told me.

Adams: Do you know what the approximate dates were?

Smith: It was winter, I do recall that, but I can't really say the exact date. But I know that it was winter.

Adams: Now you say that he purchased you two leather coats. Was it different type coats?

Smith: No, it was the same coat. What had happened was, I . . . it was very cold and I needed a winter coat, so Mr. Martin said that he would loan me the money to buy the coat, and I would pay him back in installments. So we just happened to be walking through the mall, he was there shopping, and I saw the coat. So I went in to inquire about it and found out how much it was, and at that point he purchased it.

Adams: How about the second coat? How did it come about that he purchased you a second coat?

Smith: The second coat was because the first coat I had to sell. And the second coat was about $150 cheaper, as I recall.

Adams: What was the period of time between the time the Defendant purchased this first coat and the second coat, approximately?

Smith: I would surmise perhaps two to three weeks, though I'm not sure about that. But it wasn't more than a month.

At that point, Smith was shown two receipts, which he identified as those for the coats. The prices were $317.99 and $275.59. The dates were shown to be October 11 for the first purchase and November 29 for the latter purchase.

Adams: What other pieces of personal property did the Defendant purchase for you?

Smith: That was all that he purchased for me, including the necklace and bracelet.

Adams: And the necklace and bracelet, do you know where they were purchased?

Smith: At the new mall at the pagoda, I believe, in the middle of the mall. Now the name of it, I don't recall, but I know it was one of those jewelry pagodas out there.

Adams: What kind of necklace was purchased?

Smith: A silver filigree necklace and a silver filigree bracelet that matched it.

Adams: Do you know how these purchases were accomplished?

Smith: With a credit card.

Adams: And do you know whose credit card it was?

Smith: I think it was his mother's.

Adams: Did you witness the Defendant present his mother's card for payment at Belk's?

Smith: No, I didn't witness him present the card. I was in another part of the store and simply saw him sitting over at the counter carrying on a conversation with the saleslady, and when he emerged from there, he had them.

Adams: Did you ever see any sales slip for these purchases made at Belk's?

Smith: Yes.

At that point, a Belk's receipt for $461.31, State Exhibit 31, was shown to Smith, who identified it as the receipt in question.

Adams: The jewelry that was purchased at Belk's, did you receive that jewelry?

Smith: No, it was not given to me personally.

Adams: Did you come into possession of it any time for any reason?

Smith: Yes.

Adams: For what reason did you come into possession of it?

Smith: To take it to the gold dealer or a pawn shop, as Mr. Martin asked me to do.

Adams: All right. And what request was made of you by Mr. Martin in regards to the jewelry he had purchased at Belk?

Smith: To sell it and get money for him.

Adams: Did you attempt to accommodate his wishes?

Smith: I did.

Adams: Did you take property that had been bought by Mr. Martin and try to help him sell it?

Smith: I did.

Adams: Did you go with Mr. Martin when he himself would take property he'd purchased at Belk's and other places and sell it?

Smith: I have taken Mr. Martin to various places to sell jewelry, yes.

Adams: And what kind of jewelry would it be?

Smith: Usually gold necklaces.

Adams: Where would you and he go?

Smith: He asked me to take him to a pawn shop on White Bluff. I think we went down to Habersham and Broughton, to Highway 21 in Garden City and a few others that I don't readily recall, but I'd taken him to four or five places.

Adams: Did you ever ask Mr. Martin why he was purchasing jewelry at Belk's and then taking it to a pawn shop or gold dealer and selling it?

Smith: I did question him about that, yes.

Adams: Did he respond to you?

Smith: Well, he simply said, "Don't worry about it." It was his money and he could do with it as he wished.

Adams: Did Mr. Martin ever share any of the proceeds of the money he got from selling this jewelry?

Smith: What do you mean?

Adams: Did he ever give you any of the money that he got from selling the jewelry?

Smith: Of course. I was using my car, and I needed gas.

Adams: Did Mr. Martin drive?

Smith: Not to my knowledge. He may have driven, but I've never seen him behind the wheel of a car.

Adams: When you and he would go different places together, how would you go?

Smith: I had a . . . I was purchasing a car from a mutual friend of Mr. Martin's, and, therefore, whenever he needed to go somewhere, after his father's death, I would . . . was the one to take him because his father was no longer there to give him rides.

Adams: When Mr. Martin would make contact with you, how often would it be for the purpose of providing transportation?

Smith: In the later part of our relationship, Mr. Martin would call me almost every day.

Adams: And when he would call you, how often would it be for the purpose of getting you to take him somewhere?

Smith: That was his only reason for calling me. He needed a ride.

Adams: Did you ever have an occasion where Mr. Martin would ask you to transport certain items of furniture?

Smith: Yes, sir.

Adams: Did you do that?

Smith: Yes, sir.

Adams: And where would the furniture come from?

Smith: From Mr. Martin's home.

Adams: When would you take this furniture and where would you take it?

Smith: To various antique dealers around town, Blatner's, Miss Nellie's and places like that that bought old furniture.

Adams: Do you remember any particular pieces of furniture that you took?

Smith: Well, we took wagons, small tables, a chest of drawers . . . a baby crib of some sort as I recall.

Adams: Now do you recall the date that the body of Reverend Alva Martin was discovered?

Smith: Yes.

Adams: That was on December 19, 1991.

Smith: Yes.

Adams: And you were advised of that fact, were you not, by the Chatham County Police Department?

Smith: Yes, sir.

Adams: Now, going back from December 19

to December 10, which the evidence in this case shows was the time of death, do you recall noticing any change in the behavior or manner of the Defendant during that span of time?

Smith: Well, he began to spend prolonged hours at my apartment, which was unusual, because normally he would call me and I would go pick him up, and if he came to town, he would come and say, "I need a ride," and I would take him where he needed to go. Then he would immediately, upon taking care of his business, ask me to take him home, which I did.

Adams: When you would help the defendant run these errands or when you would provide transportation for him, did it appear that he had to be at certain places at certain times?

Smith: Mr. Martin always asked me to pick him up at two o'clock, usually because I slept. I worked at night, so I slept rather late. But at two o'clock, he usually rang me up and I would go to his house and pick him up, and whatever errands he had to run, they usually had to be finished by five-thirty or six o'clock because he said he always had to be home for dinner at six.

Adams: After December 10, 1991, did that routine change?

Smith: Yes, it did. He began popping up at my apartment at odd times that were not usual. Usually he'd come, as I said, early in the day. I'd run his errands for him. But then he started to come at four and five o'clock in the afternoon and just linger. And, you know, sometimes I would ask him, "Please let me take you home now because I'm tired; I need to get some sleep; I have to go to work."

Adams: Was there any change in the time that the Defendant would remain at your home in the evening?

Smith: Indeed. I told you he started staying longer, sometimes two and three hours, sometimes several hours, at my apartment.

Adams: Now when you would go over and pick up the Defendant, did you ever notice an automobile about the premises?

Smith: Yes, sir. I think it was a Buick. It was a GM car, white, I think. Belonged to his mother and father.

Adams: Did you ever see the victim in this case operating that automobile?

Smith: Yes, I've seen Mrs. Martin drive away from her home. Yes.

Adams: When you went to pick up Mr. Martin on these various occasions, were you ever invited into the home while his mother was there?

Smith: When I went to help him move a heavy piece of furniture, on that occasion his mother was home, and I was in the house. Yes.

Adams: Was it normal for you to go in the home when you would go over to pick up Mr. Martin?

Smith: No, it was not normal.

Adams: What would you do when you would go pick him up if he were not ready at the time?

Smith: I normally would sit in front of the house in my car, listening to the radio and smoking a cigarette, waiting for him to come out. Or I would sit out in the back yard under a tree in a couple of chairs they had out there and wait for him to come out.

Adams: Between December 10, 1991 and December 19, 1991, did you notice anything that appeared unusual about the automobile that you have described as being the automobile of Mrs. Martin?

Smith: It had not been moved for quite a while, and I questioned him about his mother's mode of transportation because I knew her to drive her car away from home, after I got to know him on a daily basis. And I noticed that it hadn't been moved. And so I said, "How's your mother?" and he said that "she's fine." He said that a friend of his mother's had fallen and broke her hip and that his mother had gone to take care of her. And I then asked him how did she get there, because I knew she always drove, and he said to me that the party who broke their hip had come to pick her up, which I thought was an inconsistency, but I didn't say anything about it because I just took him at his word.

Adams: Did you have any other conversations during this nine-day period concerning his mother?

Smith: Yes I did. I had not seen his mother, and normally when I call, she would answer the phone, always, usually. And I asked him how she was and he said she was fine. I found it quite strange that the car had not been moved and that I had not seen his mother. So, I said to him that if he didn't . . . if I didn't see his mother the next afternoon, that I was going to inform the officials that I had not seen his mother. At that point, he simply said, "What's the matter with you," you know, "why are you so concerned? My mother is fine." And he seemed pretty sincere about it, so we got back into the car and I drove him on to his apartment and I went on to mine.

Adams: Where did this conversation take place?

Smith: At the Circle K.

Adams: Did you have occasion to be at the residence of Alva Martin on December 19, the day her body was discovered?

Smith: Yes, I was. I believe it was between two-thirty and three in the afternoon. Mr. Martin had called me and asked me to come and help him move some furniture. And I explained to him that I had business of my own to attend to and I could not come there. And, so, later on, after I had taken care of my business, I called Mr. Martin to see if he'd expedited his business. He wasn't home when I first called. Then he called me up and asked me to pick him up at the corner of Victory Drive and Skidaway, which I went and did. I took him home.

Adams: Did you see the Defendant any other time that day?

Smith: Yes, he called me back again and asked me to come to his apartment, and I went. It was probably about four o'clock. I'm not sure about that now, but it was late in the evening.

Adams: When you arrived, did you see the Defendant?

Smith: Yes, he was standing in the driveway.

Adams: Was there anything around him that appeared out of the ordinary?

Smith: The television, floor model TV, was sitting out there with him. He asked me to take the

TV for him and sell it.

Adams: Did you accommodate him?

Smith: I was going to, but the TV would not fit into my car. I explained to him . . . well, you see, I really didn't want to carry him with the television anyway, so I explained to him that it wouldn't fit in the car and that I couldn't help him with that, and I was sorry and I was going to leave because there was nothing I could do.

Adams: What, if anything, did the Defendant do?

Smith: He immediately began to drag the TV back toward the house, and I said, "Let me help you," and I carried it to the back door entrance and set it down.

Adams: Once you got to the back door, did you observe anything on the door out of the ordinary?

Smith: There was a note on the door, yes. I glanced at it. I mean, I didn't read the whole note. But it was like he was telling his mother where he was going and what time he would be home.

Adams: Had you seen that note prior to December 19?

Smith: The note had been there for several days.

Adams: Did that strike you as odd in any manner?

Smith: In the beginning it did not, but after seeing the same note hanging there for a couple of days, I began to think, you know, that it was odd, yes.

Adams: Had you ever seen the Defendant leave notes for his mother previous to this?

Smith: Yes. There was a ... like a chalkboard or maybe a particleboard in their entrance in the kitchen where he would normally stick the notes on there, or leave them on the table, which was right by the door as you entered.

Adams: Had you ever seen the Defendant leave a note for his mother outside on the door as it was December 19 and several days before?

Smith: No, sir.

Adams: While you were there and helping get this TV back toward the house, did you make any requests of the Defendant?

Smith: I had to urinate, and I requested that I go to the bathroom, yes.

Adams: On occasion when you've been there before and Mrs. Martin wasn't at home, had you ever made such a request?

Smith: Yes, it was granted.

Adams: What happened on this day?

Smith: Well, we sat the TV down and I realized that I had to urinate, and I reached for the screen with my right hand, and I reached for the doorknob with my left hand, and I turned it and the door began to open, and Mr. Martin just threw himself upon the door and said, "No, you can't come into my house anymore. My momma told me don't let you in here." So I thought, well, you know, it was kind of strange, but I said okay.

Adams: Did you make any observations at that point in time that raised your suspicions?

Smith: I asked him why the house smelled peculiar, and he said that it was winter and he, since his mother wasn't home, he had brought the cats in out of the trailer, and he hadn't cleaned the litter box. I accepted that. I thought it was peculiar that the litter box was smelling so strongly, but still, you know, he said that's what it was, and I couldn't tell him that it wasn't, so I just thought that it was extremely a strong odor for a cat box.

Adams: I hand you what has been marked State Exhibit 35 and ask if you can identify that exhibit.

Smith: These are the necklaces at the Piercing Pagoda.

Adams: And included in that is the necklace that you've testified that was purchased by Mr. Martin for yourself?

Smith: Sterling silver, yes.

Adams: What was the date of purchase?

Smith: November 20, 1991.

Adams: Did you ever have occasion to talk to the Defendant and discuss with him his relationship with his mother?

Smith: Mr. Martin and I discussed various things, and one of them was his relationship with his mother, yes. It appeared from what he told me that Mr. Martin and his mother had had somewhat of a tug of war as he grew up and became a man, that she was constantly having him do things that he refused . . . that he didn't really want to do, but he had no choice and . . . he had no choice but to do whatever his mother said, and he resented that. Which is what he told me, of course.

Adams: Did you have any conversations with the Defendant between the time that his father died and the time of the death of his mother regarding the relationship with his mother?

Smith: Yes, I drove him to the funeral parlor

on the night that his father was buried . . . well, shown, set out to be viewed.

Adams: After the father was buried and before his mother died, did you have any conversations with the Defendant about his relationship with his mother?

Smith: Yes, lots of just, you know, riling against authority, how he thought that all the things that had happened to him as a kid just wasn't fair, and that if she didn't stop bothering him, he was going to "f" her up.

Adams: Did he ever threaten his mother in addition to what you've just testified?

Smith: Not in my presence, but to . . . I mean, I didn't see him say this to his mother. He was saying this to me.

Adams: Did he ever tell you anything that he might do to his mother other than that?

Smith: Well, one night Mr. Martin and I was driving in my car and he began to talk—and of course I normally just listened because I didn't have much to say about it—and he suggested that if his mother kept after him that he would bash her head in.

Adams: Did Mr. Martin use the words "if she keeps after me?"

Smith: No, that's the way I'm putting it. He just, you know, was saying how he thought he was a grown man, he should have his own privileges, and his mother shouldn't run his life and . . . and that if she kept, you know, badgering him about things, that he was getting tired of it, and if "the bitch didn't leave him alone that he would kill her."

Adams: At what point in time did you know

Mrs. Martin was dead?

Smith: I knew it when the detective told me that Thursday night after I had left the house that day. I had some inkling that something was wrong that day, but I didn't know exactly what it was. I just felt that something out of the ordinary had taken place, because Mr. Martin was acting very strange, and then I smelled the peculiar odor and . . . you know, I just felt something was wrong.

Adams: Mr. Smith, how tall are you?

Smith: Five-foot, seven inches.

Adams: And what do you weigh?

Smith: One hundred twenty-six and a half pounds.

Adams: Has your height or weight fluctuated to any great degree during the time you've known the Defendant?

Smith: When I was sixteen years old, I was five-foot, seven inches, one hundred twenty-six and a half pounds. I'm thirty-seven years old and five-foot, seven inches, one hundred twenty-six and a half pounds.

Adams: Mr. Smith, did you kill Alva Martin?

Smith: No, I did not.

Adams: Did you have anything to do with the death of Alva Martin?

Smith: I had nothing to do with the death of Mrs. Martin. I simply gave Mr. Martin rides, as he requested.

Bill Dowell cross-examined Smith and educed the confession that Smith had done more than give Martin rides: that he had supplied him with crack cocaine. Excerpts of that questioning:

Dowell: You gave him rides. Was that the

entire extent of your relationship with Mr. Martin?

Smith: That was basically what we did. I went to pick him up, took him where he needed to go, and brought him back when he was ready to return.

Dowell: Your name is Larry Eugene Smith?

Smith: My name is Larry Eugene Smith.

Dowell: Are you known by other names?

Smith: I'm known by Latrice Boudoir.

Dowell: Is that your alter ego?

Smith: No, when I was very young, I was a female impersonator, and my name is Larry, so we dropped the first letters . . . the last letters, and added t-r-i-c-e to correspond to the effeminate gender.

Dowell: Now, your entire relationship was just giving Mr. Martin rides? You'd never aided him in getting crack cocaine?

Smith: I have purchased cocaine for Mr. Martin, yes.

Dowell: Taken him to buy it? You actually negotiated and purchased it for him, didn't you?

Smith: I have purchased cocaine for Mr. Martin, yes.

Dowell: How many times, Mr. Smith?

Smith: I don't recall. Mr. Martin was by my house on various occasions for that purpose. But I don't recall how many times, actually.

Dowell: Well, you've been able to recall the purchase of necklaces and how much they cost.

Smith: It was more than several (times).

Dowell: For a period of two years?

Smith: Over the period of time I've known him.

Dowell: Fifty, sixty, seventy times?

Smith: I don't think it was that many. It could have been, but I'm not sure how many times. My relationship with Mr. Martin (was) at the latter part of 1991, when I saw him mostly. I . . . he . . . was accompanying friends of mine around places that I was or at my home from time to time, but we were not bosom buddies for all the time that I've known him.

Dowell: How did you originally meet Mr. Martin? Who introduced you?

Smith: Mr. Faucette.

Dowell: Jesse Faucette?

Smith: Yes.

Dowell: And I believe you purchased cocaine for both Mr. Martin and Mr. Faucette, is that correct? That's how Mr. Martin actually got introduced to the drug, isn't it?

Smith: I don't know how Mr. Martin got introduced to the drugs. I know that Mr. Martin and Mr. Faucette came and asked me if I knew where to acquire it.

Dowell: Well, you were Mr. Martin's sole source for the drug, weren't you?

Smith: I was not Mr. Martin's sole source for that drug. I was Mr. Martin's transportation to the source of that drug.

Dowell: And once you got there, you negotiated the deals for him, didn't you?

Smith: I would go and make the purchases, yes.

Dowell: And you also partake in these drugs, didn't you?

Smith: Occasionally, yes.

Dowell: You benefited, so when you said the only way you benefited from Mr. Martin was him buying you gas, that wasn't quite the whole truth, was it?

Smith: I never said that.

Dowell: Well, excuse me, I thought when the District Attorney asked you how you benefited from selling the jewelry for Mr. Martin, you said "personally," and then he said "in any manner" and you said "from buying gas."

Smith: That's what he asked me. He didn't ask me anything about drugs.

Dowell: So you interpreted that because you purchased the drugs with this money, that didn't apply to his question when he asked you how you benefited?

Smith: Correct.

Dowell: That's a convenient interpretation.

At that point, an objection by the prosecution was sustained. Dowell then attacked the question as to why Martin bought the coats and jewelry for Smith.

Smith said, "Mr. Martin said that he was loaning me the money because that's what I asked for. It was a loan. These were not gifts. (Because) Mr. Martin was arrested, I have not repaid Mr. Martin any of that money."

Dowell then proceeded to unearth an old felony conviction against Smith stemming from 1980. Over objections from the Prosecution, Dowell attempted to impeach the Smith's testimony by waving the felony history before the jury.

Smith confessed that he had pleaded guilty to the charge of robbery by intimidation, and affirmed

Dowell's statement that Smith had been sentenced to three years in jail, of which he actually served seven months. However, he contended that he was "set up."

Dowell attempted to get Smith to confess to partaking in smoking crack cocaine with his customers, which Smith repeatedly denied.

"Mr. Martin paid me in cash (for services such as transportation and drug transactions). Whatever I did with it was my business."

Obviously, any efforts to discredit Smith's testimony did not sway the jury, although, an objective look at the other circumstantial evidence—even without Smith's statements—seems likely to brought about a conviction anyway.

In redirect, the Prosecution established that Smith had been told "to be truthful with all the information asked of me" if he were questioned about supplying drugs.

He was also asked about instructions he had received regarding testimony about the use and consumption of the drugs by Jim Martin.

"I was instructed to tell the truth, and not to mention that unless I was asked," he said.

Finally, he was shown a note that allegedly listed the debts that Larry Smith had incurred to Jim Martin through "loans." He said that he had seen Martin "write that down" on the paper.

After numerous objections from the Defense, which apparently regarded the note as evidence that would support Smith's testimony about his relationship with the Defendant, the note was ultimately admitted into evidence.

Barbara Perry was next to testify. The first

thing the Prosecution re-established through Perry was Alva Martin's routine.

"Very precise, very rigid, everything was on schedule regardless," she said when asked to describe Alva Martin's daily routine. 'She had her schedule whether somebody came to the house or not. She went to the grocery store every day around four, between four and four-thirty, Monday through Friday, without fail."

The questioning then shifted to the visit by the Perrys to the Martin house on October 15, 1991. At the request of Robert Perry's sister, Hilda Donaldson, Mrs. Perry had telephoned Alva Martin on October 14. Alva requested that they visit "to talk to her and Jimmy." The Perrys traveled from their rural Georgia home to Savannah the following day.

Barbara Perry testified, when asked if she had had a conversation with Jim Martin about his relationship with his mother, "I told him . . . for him not to do anything that would hurt his mother."

The conversation then adjourned to the outside of the house, privately between Jim and his aunt.

"We talked about some of the problems, and also the little things that had happened during the past in his upbringing and things like that, and also that I felt like that he needed to seek counseling. I recommended it to him. At the time he told me that he had made an appointment at Charter (an addiction-treatment facility), but that he had cancelled it."

Again in November, Hilda Donaldson asked Mrs. Perry to contact Mrs. Martin. She called Alva on the morning of November 10. The result of the conversation led to another trip for the Perrys to Savannah. They arrived on Sunday morning. The main topic of discussion was the use of Alva's credit cards.

Perry testified, "I asked him about using the charge cards, and he kind of smiled and looked at me. 'Because I had been told the cards were destroyed.' And I asked him, 'They sent new cards to the house didn't they?' and Jimmy kind of smiled at me, and I said, 'You took them out of the mailbox, didn't you?' and Jimmy replied, 'Yes.'"

Did he offer justification?

"He said, 'I hate everything you (Alva) stand for,' was the reason for what he had done."

Again, Perry said, aunt and nephew moved outdoors for a private conversation.

"I talked to him about selling some of the things that were in the house. I mentioned the piano, and he said, well, that was his piano. He said he was using it (the money from selling items) to buy some things for Jesse and for Larry, that he had bought two leather coats for Larry and some jewelry, and he'd bought some jewelry for Jesse. After that conversation, we went back inside. We had talked about him going to Georgia Regional for some treatments and he said that he did not want to go and stay, that he would go as an out-patient."

She said that Jim, however, reversed himself once the conversation moved back inside. "He had a change of attitude once we got inside. He said he wouldn't go."

The last time she saw or had any contact with Alva Martin, Barbara Perry testified, was on

November 28, 1991, Thanksgiving Day. On December 11, the day after the established date of Alva's murder, Mrs. Perry had called the Martin house.

"Jimmy answered. He said she was not home, that she had been staying with a friend that had broken her hip, someone by the name of Anita, that she'd been staying with her for a week, taking care of her. He said that he missed his mother not being at home, and that she had told him that she wanted us to come by on Christmas to visit them, and that she planned to make us some brownies."

That was the last time she spoke to Jim until after his arrest.

The next time would make headlines.

When she learned of Alva's death, Barbara Perry testified that she went to the police station on Hodgson Memorial in Savannah. Asked if she had contact with the Defendant, she replied that she had received a phone call.

"He (Jim) called me. His first statement to me was, 'Barbara, I killed her. Larry made me do it. Larry did it.'"

"Have you had occasion to visit with the Defendant since he has been incarcerated?" she was asked.

"Yes, I have. He told me he did not kill her. He said that Larry came in the house with him one evening, and that they were going to discuss . . . that they were going to try to pay off some money, and that Larry grabbed her before he realized what was happening and had started strangling her."

After establishing that Jim had said he was there and did nothing to prevent the strangulation, the Prosecution asked if he had said why he did not try to prevent the murder of his mother.

"I asked him why he didn't try to fight or stop it, and he said he was afraid, that Larry had threatened him."

Asked about Alva's body being wrapped in blankets and tied, she responded "He said Larry made him do it."

Interestingly, Adams' next questions concerned Alva Martin's standard of living.

"She had approximately two hundred coming in from Social Security and just a little less than three hundred from my brother's retirement, which would have been a little less than five hundred a month. This was very hard on her, because she had never had to live that way. My brother had a good income, and she was not expecting it to be this way."

Was she struggling financially?

"Yes, she was. I had made several trips in October to help her to be able to get food stamps and some help in that way."

Barbara Perry also testified that Alva wore limited jewelry—a wedding ring and lapel pins "but other than that no jewelry"—and that she wore scarves most of the time. "That was one of her trademarks."

The Prosecution wound up its questioning with inquiries about the relationship between aunt and nephew.

"Mrs. Perry, are you still visiting the Defendant in jail?"

"Yes, I am. I've been to see him once every two weeks since he's been there. I'm still concerned about him and his welfare. I love him."

On cross-examination, Dowell attempted to portray Martin as a dominated, mistreated child who would follow the lead of anyone who led him, including Larry Smith. "I think Larry took over where Alva left off," Perry testified toward the end of Dowell's questioning.

On Jim Martin's upbringing: "(It was) very, very rigid. He was never allowed to be a little boy. He was never allowed to make any decisions for himself whatsoever. He was never allowed to listen to any music or read any magazines that were not religious or church related. He was never allowed to have toys that little boys played with. He had to do exactly as she said."

She agreed with Dowell's terminology that Alva was "domineering," and when asked how Alva treated her husband, Emerson Martin's sister answered, "The same way."

Testimony about Emerson's final days of life illustrated Alva's attitude.

"I believe you related to me an instance when his father was on his death bed," Dowell said.

"Yes, Jimmy wanted to stay at the hospital with me, because his father was very critical. And she (Alva) said, 'I'm sorry,' that she needed to get some rest, and Jimmy had to go home with her. He said, 'I would like to stay with my daddy and Barbara,' but he wasn't allowed to."

Perry agreed with Dowell's questions that Jim Martin was "easily influenced by others," and that "someone could manipulate him." When asked if she would describe Jim as being aggressive or passive, she answered, "Passive."

In regard to the charge cards, the Prosecution had painted the picture that Jim had used the cards not only to get money to buy drugs, but also as an angry and rebellious answer to his mother's values.

"I don't feel he was angry," Barbara Perry testified.

Was Alva angry? Dowell asked.

"She was disappointed." Perry agreed with Dowell's suggestion that the credit card incidents themselves did not threaten the relationship between mother and son.

"Now as far as (Jim seeking treatment) the Georgia Regional thing, he originally agreed to go, is that correct?" Dowell asked.

"Yes, he did."

"But what was the stipulation he told you?"

"He wanted his mother to go with him to the sessions, to the counseling."

"And ultimately did both agree?"

"No."

"Was that the reason for his change in attitude and reason for not going?"

"Yes."

As to the story of Jim telling people that his mother was nursing a sick friend, Barbara Perry said that, "He had a vivid imagination." But she also said, "I think he could have been led into it (telling that story)."

Dowell asked, "Were you familiar as far as what influence Larry Smith had over Jim, from talking to him or from personally observing the situation?"

"I think Larry took over where Alva left off."

As to the fact that Jim Martin had little to no

reaction on the night of the discovery of his mother's body, Mrs. Perry said, "He was not allowed to show his emotions (when he was a child). The family was never allowed to show emotion."

"Was it like that when his father died also?"

"No, that was a different case. He was very upset over his father's death."

"But as far as his mother was concerned, you would not be surprised if someone told you that he was not emotional when he was informed of his mother's death?"

"No," Barbara Perry said simply, and her testimony was finished for the time being, although she would later be recalled by the State as a rebuttal witness after her nephew's testimony.

Owen Ferguson was the last witness for the State. At the time he took the stand, Ferguson said that he had been a police officer for twenty-three years, seventeen of those with Chatham County.

After another brief round of questioning over Miranda rights and Jim Martin's signing of the waiver, Adams asked Ferguson about Martin's response to the news of his mother's murder.

"He said, yes, we need to talk about that,'" Ferguson testified. "I then asked him why did he kill his mother? He showed no emotions and just sort of laughingly says, 'Well, I didn't do that. Larry did it.' And he went on to say that Larry used a necktie around her neck. He claimed that Larry made him wrap her up in a blanket and tie her up like a pig and hide her into a closet. He gave the reasons why, was to steal property and purchase cocaine and the misuse of credit cards and things of this nature. At this particular time, I was going to record it, and he says, 'I think I need my attorney—I need to talk to a lawyer,' was his words. At that time, the interview was stopped."

Ferguson said that Martin confirmed the date of Alva's death to be December 10.

"Did you conduct an interview of Larry Smith?" Adams asked.

"Yes, sir, I did. He gave me a statement."

"You have heard today the testimony of Larry Smith on the stand . . . is that consistent with the statement that was given to you . . . when you interviewed him?"

"Yes, sir, it is," Ferguson said. "Mr. Smith was interviewed that same morning December 20. The homicide . . . we found the body on the nineteenth, but after midnight, we'll use the calendar date of the twentieth."

"Other than the statement of the Defendant that Larry Smith was involved in the homicide, have you uncovered any evidence that Larry Smith was either the participant of this homicide or that he in any manner was a party to it?"

"None whatsoever," Ferguson concluded.

Upon cross-examination by Dowell, Ferguson said that he did not ask or try to determine the whereabouts of Larry Smith on December 10, the night that Alva Martin was killed. He said that while Larry Smith did talk "about getting capital" from being Jim's errand boy, he had not talked openly about the purchase of drugs.

At that point, the Prosecution rested its case. The Defense had only one witness, the Defendant. His testimony:

Dowell: Jim, do you know why you're here

today?

Martin: Yes, sir, I do.

Dowell: You're being charged and tried for the death of your mother, Alva Mize Martin.

Martin: Yes, sir.

Dowell: Did you kill your mother?

Martin: No, sir, I did not.

Dowell: Who killed your mother?

Martin: Larry Eugene Smith.

Dowell: How did he kill your mother?

Martin: He strangled her with a necktie he had taken from out of my bedroom.

Dowell: You heard testimony concerning that bandanna which has been admitted into evidence. Was that how he killed your mother?

Martin: No, sir, there was a long necktie that he put around her neck.

Dowell: Take us back to that day of December 10 . . . why did Larry come over to the house?

Martin: He called me on the phone that night. I'd seen him earlier that day. He said that he wanted to come over and talk to me, and I said okay. So when he arrived, he came and knocked on the door of my trailer and I let him in, and he began a conversation with me concerning how we needed to talk with my mother about the charges that we had made on the credit cards, and to find a way to start making restitution for the monies that we had spent. And he wanted to go inside and talk to her about it. So we went into the house. I went into my room to get something. I don't know whether it was a statement or a bill or a receipt of something that I wanted to get. And when I came back into the living room, I went and looked out the front window of the house, and when I looked back, he was standing behind her at the chair, and her head was over like this, and it was blood coming out of her mouth. And I tried to get to the telephone at this point. I jumped or leaped across the living room as fast as I could and grabbed the phone. He knocked the phone out of my hand and pulled a knife on me. I've since been told it's a butterfly knife. It's a long knife, and you flip the handle, and it makes an extension about like this. And he pinned me to the floor, he knocked me to the floor and said that if I told anybody about this, if I didn't do what he said from then on in, that he was going to kill me, and he would burn our house down, and no one would ever know what happened to me or my mother."

Dowell: Did he threaten to harm anyone else?

Martin: Well, yes, he did. (He said) if I told anyone or if I told Jesse, he would kill him, too."

Dowell: Now, Jesse is the person you were having a relationship at that time with?

Martin: Yes, sir.

Dowell: After he threatened you not to tell anyone, what happened then?

Martin: He left the necktie around her neck and took the body out of the chair and drug it down the hall and he looked around in the back of the house. I don't know. He wanted to know what the back hall closet was. I told him it was a dirty clothes closet where, you know, we kept our . . . there was a rollaway bed in there and a dirty clothes hamper and stuff like that. And so he moved the stuff out of the closet. He then proceeded to tier her hands together, her ankles together, and he gagged her with the bandanna that was later found around her neck, and put her in the closet, pushed her in the closet in pretty much of a sitting position."

Dowell: How did he get her from the chair to the closet?

Martin: He pulled her by her feet.

Dowell: When he pulled her by her feet, did her head hit anything?

Martin: Yes, sir, it hit the floor. And like I said, he drug her down the hall, looked around the back part of the house. He wanted to know what the closet was. I opened it and showed it to him. And he tied her as I described and put her in the closet. He went through her pocketbook that was in her bedroom, and there was some money in there, about ten or twenty dollars. And she'd just gotten a book of food stamps. And he took all of that and took me back downtown and purchased crack."

Dowell: What happened then?

Martin: He gave me some of it and took me home.

Dowell: When did you first meet Larry?

Martin: I knew who he was off and on since I was a teenager from just seeing him around town, but I hadn't really met him to know him personally until about two years ago.

Dowell: When you first saw him, first met him, did he appear to be a male or a female at that time?

Martin: A male.

Dowell: Did you ever know him as his alter ego or other personality?

Martin: Yes, I did. That was, like I described, when I first encountered him out and about I would see him, he would be dressed as a woman.

Dowell: Did you in fact connect him with being the woman that you knew when you first met him?

Martin: Pretty much. I didn't know that his name was Larry Smith. You know, I knew him as Latrice then, or knew that was his name.

Dowell: And who introduced you to him?

Martin: Jesse and other friend, Jeff, took me over to Larry's apartment.

Dowell: And what was the purpose for going over to Larry's apartment?

Martin: They wanted to buy some pot from Larry, some marijuana, and he had small amounts of it in little plastic envelopes that he sold for ten dollars each.

Dowell: And basically, that was the main reason for seeing Larry?

Martin: Yes, sir.

Dowell: Did you and Jesse continue to see Larry under those circumstances?

Martin: Yes, sir, we did from time to time.

Dowell: For how long?

Martin: I would say at least a good year to year and a half.

Dowell: When did you first get introduced to crack cocaine?

Martin: It was sometime in the early summer of 1991, sometime around June, as near as I can pinpoint it.

Dowell: And who introduced you to it?

Martin: Jesse, actually.

Dowell: And where did he get the crack?

Martin: He had bought it from Larry, or he

gave Larry money, and Larry had gone and bought it. Whatever, you know.

Dowell: What was your reaction when you first smoked it?

Martin: It was like nothing else I'd ever encountered in my life. I'd taken one form or drug or another since I'd been a child. When I was a child, my mom gave me tranquilizers and sleeping pills to help me sleep. She gave me her medicine that she was using at the same time.

At that point, testimony was interrupted, and Barbara Perry was asked to leave the courtroom. The Prosecution stated that it might be necessary to recall Mrs. Perry to rebut some part of her nephew's testimony.

Martin: She needed them (the pills) to help her sleep, and I was hyperactive, I guess, as a child. I had trouble going to sleep, trouble falling asleep. And she would take a whole pill and give me half of a pill. So, I was about six or seven when this happened. And from then on, (it was like that). When I was a young teenager, my dad had a severe heart attack. And at that particular time, doctors were giving prescriptions for a lot of controlled substances which they don't give you now, such as Quaaludes and Seconals and Demerols for heart pain, and my dad would give those to my mother and I to help us sleep. So I had been taking one thing or another since I was very small."

Dowell: So your reaction to crack was what?

Martin: Well it was, like I said, it was like nothing else I'd ever had in my life. Anything else, it was like, you could put it down, you really didn't need it, it was okay. But this was something that, once I had smoked just one time of it, I was hooked on it. I couldn't do anything about it except want to get more of it. It created an immediate craving like nothing else I've ever had.

Dowell: Were you working at the time?

Martin: Yes, sir, I was.

Dowell: After you smoked it the first time, when was the next time you bought it?

Martin: Probably the next night.

Dowell: Who did you buy it from?

Martin: From Larry.

Dowell: Did Larry actually sell it to you, or was he the medium through which you purchased it?

Martin: I would give Larry money, and he would go to one of various locations and get it. He knew several people around town that he could get it from.

Dowell: Did you ever purchase it on your own?

Martin: No sir, I attempted to do that one time, and in fact, went to an individual in a neighborhood where we'd been earlier in the evening and bought twenty dollars' worth of crack, and . . . .

Dowell: When you say, "we," who?

Martin: Jesse and I. And we went back to the same individual later that night and gave him twenty dollars.

Dowell: You said Jesse and you. Did Larry accompany you when you first purchased it?

Martin: At first, yes, and we got some. And then we said, well, we'd go back by ourselves, just to see how it would be. And so we went and found the same guy and gave him twenty dollars. And he went up to a little house that was there and said, "I'll be right back in a minute." And what we found out later is he actually broke a piece of the brick off of a house and came and handed it to us. By the time we saw what it was, he was running down the street. So from then on, if you wanted to get it, there was only one way to get it, and that was with Larry's help.

Dowell: So you continued to purchase through Larry?

Martin: Yes, sir.

Dowell: You heard people talk about, or you heard the testimony about the coats you bought him and the jewelry you bought him. Why did you buy these articles for him?

Martin: He asked me to. He found things that he wanted and told me that he wanted them, and I felt like if I didn't do what he said that, I don't know whether he would harm me or . . . or what. But anyway, I felt like that I was under his control. I would do, you know, whatever it took to please him.

Dowell: You heard him testify that these were loans. Were these in fact loans to him?

Martin: Some mention was made of paying me back, but nothing actually happened. I had initially made the little card with the prices on it, just to see what had actually been spent on him, and it was a matter of keeping a record so much as for my own self. And there was a time when I did show it to him and say, you know, "This is what I have spent, you know, on you, outside of the monies that I've given you every day."

Dowell: Did you start on crack before or after your father died?

Martin: It was before. About sometime in June, nearest I can figure.

Dowell: Did your usage increase with time or did it remain the same?

Martin: Pretty much the same. I think it got worse after my dad died.

Dowell: On the average, how much crack would you buy a week?

Martin: Maybe between three and five hundred dollars' worth.

Dowell: Was that a daily occurrence with you, (or was it) every other day, or (something else)?

Martin: Pretty much every day.

Dowell: How were you financing this habit of yours?

Martin: Various ways. There was a checking account that my mother was a custodian for, and I wrote checks out to me and had them cashed. I signed her name to them. I really didn't use the credit cards until after my dad died. And initially what I used were cards that were his.

Dowell: As far as the checks were concerned, did you ultimately tell your mother about them?

Martin: Yes, I did, about two weeks before my dad died. I tried to get away from this whole situation and re-establish myself with my family and seek help about it in a spiritual way, you know, through prayer and trying to make a new start. I sat down with my mother and father and talked to both of them about what I had done and how I wanted to get over it. I wanted to get away from it. And it seemed to work for a few days. My mother actually cashed in a certificate of deposit that she had and put the monies back in the checking account and turned the account over to someone else. And there had been an overage at the bank, for which she took out a loan and paid that off for me.

Dowell: Could you stop using crack at that time?

Martin: I did for a few days, but it really didn't take. It didn't really last.

Dowell: You were calling up Larry to come purchase crack for you, or was he calling you up?

Martin: It was both at different times. Like right about this time we're talking about here, he called me and got me to go back with him again and get some more. He hadn't heard from me in a few days. He did work, but during the time I knew him and was buying crack from him, from June until December 19, I couldn't really say he only worked about a month out of that time at a job.

Dowell: Was he benefiting from you purchasing crack?

Martin: Yes, sir. I gave him approximately twenty dollars a day cash money and also put the gas in the car on top of that. I later found out from someone that was a brother of someone we had bought from that Larry had bought the stuff for us from...."

Further testimony to that question was stopped by an objection by the Prosecution, which was sustained.

Dowell: Was he also using the crack that you purchased?

Martin: At times.

Dowell: So you were working, you were

writing checks. Did you start selling any articles?

Martin: Not at this time.

Dowell: When did you start selling your articles?

Martin: After I had tried to straighten myself out, and he'd gotten back in touch with me, and I'd started smoking again, then I left my job, and about three days after that my dad died, and, you know, it was pretty downhill all the way after that.

Dowell: What did you start selling?

Martin: Well, initially I sold things that belonged to me. I had furniture in my bedroom, furniture in my trailer. I owned two video cassette recorders. I had a compact disc player with a tape player and speakers, a Sony unit. It was real nice. I had another set of stereo components. I had a smaller stereo with a cassette player in it. I had a record collection of several thousand LP's, which I sold. I also collected antique 78 (rpm) phonograph records of opera singers and I had about, between five and seven hundred of those (which) I sold for about two hundred dollars. I had a number of books which I sold, (and) items of furniture out of my bedroom. I did sell my piano. I felt like that was mine. It had been given to me when I was thirteen by my mom and dad, and I'd played the piano and took lessons on it and had been a music major in college. So, out of the money that I got for the piano, which was four hundred and fifty dollars, I gave my mother a hundred dollars out of that to help her.

Dowell: Would it be a fair assumption to say you started selling everything you owned to buy crack?

Martin: At this point, yes.

Dowell: When did you start using your mother's credit cards?

Martin: After my dad died, I used his, and then later, there was her Belk's card and her Levy Jewelers card.

Dowell: Were you able to stop doing this?

Martin: No, sir.

Dowell: After Larry killed your mother, did he ever come back over to the house?

Martin: Yes, he did.

Dowell: How often?

Martin: Every day. He would call me on the phone. I didn't know exactly when he might show up. I was really terrified of him at this point.

Dowell: Did he help you in moving any of this furniture after your mother was killed?

Martin: Yes, he did, particularly the trunk that we moved, had to be moved out. It was in my bedroom and had to be moved down the hall and out through the living room and the back door and into the back of the station wagon.

Dowell: What about the console TV? Were you able to move that out of the house by yourself?

Martin: The console TV had rollers on the bottom of it, so you could roll it up to a certain point, but then it had to be lifted up and carried or put over into a trunk or into some type of vehicle to be transported.

Dowell: Did Larry help you do that?

Martin: He attempted to do that, and it wouldn't fit into the trunk of his car. He had had to turn in his station wagon because he hadn't been making regular payments to the man that he was getting it from, and, in fact, had rented a car that he used to transport us around, which I was making the car rental payments, too.

Dowell: On December 19, did you refuse entrance of Larry to the house?

Martin: No, sir, I did not. He came and went as he wanted to, you know. I never refused him entrance to the house.

Dowell: You heard him testify that you started coming over and staying at his house for long periods of time after December 10, between December 10 and December 19. Is that true?

Martin: There were times when he kept me with him longer, I think, and he would show up at odd moments, like three or four in the morning and take me off somewhere and do things like that, bring me back three or four hours later. He said that he couldn't sleep well at night, that from his years of when he'd been a female impersonator and worked the bars . . . . "

An objection, sustained, interrupted the testimony.

Martin: Anyway, he was used to getting to sleep at six or seven o'clock in the morning.

Dowell: Now, as far as the police coming by to check on your mother, did you tell them this story about her going to visit a friend with a broken hip?

Martin: Yes, sir. There was a lady that had broken her hip, and Larry knew about this, and he told me that if . . . . "

Again, a sustained objection stopped Martin's testimony.

Dowell: Did you think up the idea yourself, or was it furnished to you by someone else?

Martin: No, sir, I didn't think it up. It was

suggested to me by him (Larry).

Dowell: What did Larry Smith tell you to tell the police or tell anyone that inquired?

Martin: I was to tell anyone that a friend of my mother's, Anita Davis, had fallen and broken her hip. Mother had actually been to see her at Candler Hospital. A lady from Stillwell Towers supposedly came by and picked up Mother and took her to Anita's house, where she was convalescing. Anita lived on Fifty-fifth Street, I believe. And that's what I was to tell anyone that asked or made inquiry.

Dowell: Why did you tell people this? Why didn't you, when the police came by, tell them what was going on?

Martin: I don't know. I was afraid. I felt like no one would believe me. I was so under his control. I'd been smoking crack for six months on a daily basis, and it does change your perception and alter your thinking, you know.

Dowell: Well, why did you tell Detective Ferguson he (Larry) did it when you refused to tell other people (including police) when they came by?

Martin: Actually, when I met Detective Ferguson and we sat in the interview room, I felt a sense of relief. I felt like I could trust him, and that I could finally tell someone the whole story about what had happened to me.

Dowell: Now you said that Larry tied your mother's hands and ankles or wrists and ankles and put her in the closet?

Martin: Yes.

Dowell: Did she remain in that state, or did something happen to change her situation?

Martin: For about three days. On Friday of

that week, he took her body out of the closet and directed me to find some blankets or something around the house that she could be wrapped in. I felt at that time that he was going to move her body somewhere. Whether he actually said that to me or not, I don't know, but I had that idea. There was a quilt in a linen closet, and in the closet she had been in was a blanket in a box and another type quilt. And we laid them on the floor and put her on top of them, and he proceeded to remove the necktie from around her neck and wrists and ankles and actually slid the bandanna down her face. It had been knotted so tightly that he couldn't get it loose, and he left it there.

Dowell: Do you know what he did with the ties?

Martin: No, sir, I don't know.

Dowell: After he tried to remove the bandanna, what did he and you do?

Martin: We wrapped the blankets around her, and I had some hospital surgical restraint type things that I had—someone I knew had given them to me—and we looped those around the body, and there's a hole that you push it through, and you pull back on it, and that made sort of a (support) . . . at one end and at the other end and then in the middle.

Dowell: You heard Ralph Allen testify that you made threats to harm your mother to him. Is there any reason why Ralph Allen would come and testify against you?

Martin: I believe that because I wasn't able to go along with what Mr. Allen wanted me to do with him or for him.

Dowell: Enlighten us on that. What did he

want you to do?

Martin: Well, when I first went to work at the store, we were very good friends, and he took me home to have dinner with him on three occasions. He testified to two, but I remember three. Each time I would play with the children. He has a little boy and a little girl, and we'd sit on the floor and play with their toys. He had a piano in the home. We'd play the piano and sing. His wife's a really good cook, and we'd have a real good dinner. And then, when it would come time to take me home, he had Styrofoam containers in his garage, and he'd just pile a bunch of food in the containers and give them to me to take home with me. He took me to my house by himself on two occasions after dinner at his house. The first time he walked me to my trailer, and we sat the food down inside, and he sat down, and we began talking. He said he was tired or something of this nature, and I said, "Well, let me massage your feet for you." And so he took off his shoes, and I did that. It's something strictly therapeutic. I don't consider it an overture to anyone. It makes someone feel better, it stimulates the nerve endings, and it's good therapy, really. Anyway, on the second occasion when he brought me home and brought the food in, he went to leave and I hugged him. I really thought of him very fondly, like I would a brother or something like that. He'd kind of taken me under his wing, and I felt really good about him. And it was at this point that he became sexually aroused and told me to get down on my knees in front of him and to "rub my face against it, but don't take it out." And I did that. He was my boss. I didn't want to do it, but I felt like

I should do it. And then he made me turn around and—at no time did we have our clothing off—he made me turn around and bend over, and he simulated intercourse with me, and reached around and grabbed me by the chest. I had bruises for a couple of days. I mean, it wasn't really that big a deal. He never went all the way with it, but I felt like (he would have done so) if there hadn't have been this person in my life, that he really didn't care for and he used to talk against to me—Jesse is who I'm referring to. He'd met him. He'd come to the office and sit in Ralph's office and talked with him a good hour one day. And he knew about him; he knew that Jesse was abusive toward me. He occasionally would slap me around or beat me up, and I've gone to work with bruises on my face and make-up base to try to hide them or something. And he'd call me in the office and he'd say, "Jim, the make-up's not covering those bruises."

Dowell: Getting back in focus, did he ever ask you anything about Jesse? Or ask you to do anything regarding Jesse?

Martin: Well, he told me that he felt like I was having to spend a good deal of my money on Jesse, taking him to dinner and things like this or buying groceries for him. And he said, "Don't you ever want somebody that can buy some of the ice cream for you, too, Jim?" He said things like that that led me to believe that he felt like it was a bad relationship and that I should get away from him. At one point, he actually told me that he was afraid Jesse might kill me.

Dowell: Did he ask you to leave Jesse for him?

Martin: Not specifically.

Dowell: Now, you heard your aunt testify as far as the phone call you made to her at the Chatham County Police Department. How did you happen to call her there?

Martin: I don't recollect whether I called someone here in Savannah, and they told me she was there, whether I tried to call her at her residence and got no answer. I don't remember how I tracked her there, but I found out she was there, and I made the call.

Dowell: Did you ever tell her that you did it?

Martin: No, sir, I didn't.

Dowell: What did you tell her?

Martin: I told her that Larry had done it.

Dowell: Were you emotional at the time?

Martin: Very emotional. I mean I . . . it's hard to say how I might have come across. I know I was crying over the phone to her.

Dowell: Have you ever threatened to harm your mother in front of anyone?

Martin: No, sir, not at all.

Dowell: Do you love your mother?

Martin: Yes, sir, I do.

Dowell: Well, I'm sure the jury is wondering how could you cover up her death for this long?

Martin: I don't know. I've asked myself that a hundred times, you know. In the thirteen months now that I've been clean and haven't done any drugs, you see things a lot clearer in the light of day. At that time, I was afraid. I wanted to get to a point where I could get away from him, get from under his control, and tell what really happened. I don't know. I was afraid of him. I really was. I was terrified of him.

Dowell: Did you harm your mother in any way?

Martin: No, sir, I did not.

Adams' cross-examination of Martin was nearly as long as Dowell's questioning. Most of that testimony is listed here; that which is not listed is superfluous testimony, such as agreeing on dates and places. In some cases, questions or answers have been combined, although the questions might have been asked sequentially. In all such cases, the response from the Defendant was the same to all the questions asked.

Adams: I'm going to ask you a series of questions, and if you don't understand a question, you let me know, and I will rephrase the question. I don't mean to trick you in any manner, okay?

Martin: Yes, sir.

Adams: We agree that your mother was killed on December 10, 1991, that she was killed in Chatham County, Georgia, and that at the time of death you were present.

Martin: Yes, sir. I was in the house, yes.

Adams: We agree, do we not, that prior to the death of your mother, you had taken credit cards belonging to your father and issued in his name, and you had gone out and amassed a great sum of money owing on those cards, and that you did that without authorization, and that you took your mother's cards, specifically a card at Belk's, and did the same thing?

Martin: Yes, sir.

Adams: Will you agree that because of the fact that you were misusing your mother's cards, that you and your mother's relationship deteriorated?

Martin: No, sir, I can't say that.

Adams: Will you agree that when you began to sell this property that your mother did not go along with that, but you continued it anyway?

Martin: There are times I think that it hurt her and upset her. There were items of my personal furniture that she didn't want to see me sell.

Adams: She didn't want you to sell the piano, did she?

Martin: She didn't know about me selling the piano until after it happened. Obviously it was gone. And I gave her a hundred dollars of the money.

Adams: When did this occur?

Martin: Sometime in October. It was sold to Music, Inc., on Abercorn Street.

Adams: Do you know or have an idea as to how much debt you had accumulated on the credit cards at the time you sold the piano?

Martin: No, sir, I do not.

Adams: It was in the thousands of dollars, was it not?

Martin: Possibly so, yes.

Adams: Nobody forced you to smoke crack, did they?

Martin: Not initially. Someone said, "Here, try this," and I did, and that was all it took.

Adams: Now you say that on the date that your mother was killed that Larry came to your trailer and says, "Let's go in and talk to your mother about paying some bills." Is that right?

Martin: Yes, sir. He'd had a conversation with me in his automobile about two weeks before that and had not followed through on it. He said, "We need to talk to your mother about paying on her bills that we've run up here. You need to get a job or see about getting your unemployment. We need to start trying to make some restitution to her." And he didn't follow up on it till that night, when he came over and said the same thing, so I believed that's what he intended to do.

Adams: You were not employed, and I believe you testified that Larry was not employed on a regular basis, is that correct?

Martin: Not at this time.

Adams: So if neither of you were employed, how was it that you and Larry were going to get together and take care of these thousands of dollars that you'd run up on your credit cards?

Martin: Well, he wanted to make a start in that direction. It was possible for me to get my unemployment insurance. Right after my dad died—and I'd left my job just before he died—Mr. Allen had called and spoke with my mother and said that he would help me get unemployment. I never went and got it, but I could have.

Adams: It's your testimony that you went in the house and that you went into a bedroom, is that correct?

Martin: Yes, sir.

The next few questions established that the house was small, three bedrooms, a bathroom, a living room and dining area, back and front porches and a utility room off the back porch. The rooms in the house were small and close together.

Adams: So you go in the house and you go into a bedroom, and what is the next thing that you say you know is that you came back out and your mother is sitting in a chair with her head dropped over?

Martin: Yes, sir.

Adams: What room was she in?

Martin: She was really in between the living room and the dining room. There was a large easy chair there, a recliner that my dad had, that she was sitting in.

Adams: How long were you in this bedroom?

Martin: Approximately a couple of minutes. I was trying to find some receipts or something to show her and talk with her about, that I had in my bedroom.

Adams: You heard Dr. Sperry testify that at a minimum, it would take two to three minutes to strangle a person to death, did you not?

Martin: Yes, sir. I heard him testify that within ten to twenty seconds, they could lose consciousness, but actually for death to be completed, it would take that long.

Adams: And you say when you came out, you discovered this situation, and your initial reaction was to go for the phone, is that right?

Martin: Yes, sir, to try to call for help.

Adams: Did you say anything?

Martin: I don't . . . no, I don't think so. I don't remember if I did.

Adams: So you come out of the bedroom, your mother's sitting in a chair, her head is hanging over and blood is coming out of her mouth, and you don't say a word?

Martin: I jumped for the phone, to grab the phone, to call the police. I was going to dial 911.

Adams: My question is when you came out and found your mother in the condition that you have testified to, you did not say one word?

Martin: No, sir.

Adams: Now you told this jury here today that Larry Smith pulled a knife on you. Have you ever told anybody else Larry Smith pulled a knife on you? Did you tell Corporal Ferguson?

Martin: Yes, sir.

Adams: You heard Corporal Ferguson testify about the statements you gave. Did you hear any mention of any knife during his giving of that statement?

Martin: No, sir, I didn't. But I told him. Whether it was at the time of the statement or not, I don't know.

Adams: Well, if you didn't tell him at the time of the statement, when did you tell him?

Martin: I really don't know. He came in the interview room, and we started talking. I started telling him what had happened to me. He said, "Let's put it on a tape." He put the tape into the player. I started over again with my story. He said, "Hold on a minute, I want to read this to you." He began reading my rights to me over the tape. He got to the point where it said you may have a lawyer present. I said, "Well, maybe I should talk to a lawyer." He shut the tape off and said, "You're under arrest for murder," and, "Who do you want to call or do you want me to call?"

Adams: And you testified that when you got to the police station that you felt relieved? You felt, after talking with Detective Ferguson, or beginning to talk to him, that you finally had somebody that

you could tell everything to?
Martin: Yes, sir, that's true.
Adams: Well, did you tell him everything?
Martin: Pretty much. I didn't go into all the details, you know, about past history or credit cards or things like that, but as far as relating to the events surrounding the death, (yes).
Adams: Are you telling this jury that you told Detective Ferguson things that are not in the statement he read today?
Martin: I believe that when I initially spoke to him, I may have said things that aren't included in the statement. After he began formally taking the statement from me is what you have now as the statement.
Adams: And when you say you told him everything, did you tell him about the fact that (Larry) had come back over to your house every day after the death?
Martin: I don't recall that.
Adams: Well, that's part of everything, isn't it?
Martin: Not just surrounding the immediate death. No, sir. That would have been afterwards.
Adams: Did you tell Detective Ferguson that you had called people and tried to make them believe that your mother was still alive when she was laying in that closet deteriorating?
Martin: No, sir, I did not.
Adams: Is that part of everything?
Martin: Yes, sir.
Adams: In fact, you weren't so relieved to talk to Detective Ferguson, were you?
Martin: Yes, I was.

Adams: Well, then, why, if you were so relieved to talk to him, when he asked you about taping the conversation, you asked for a lawyer?

Martin: Well, after he read me that, I said I should talk to a lawyer. And he called him on the phone, and the lawyer advised me not to say anything until he came to see me the next day at the jail. And that's what happened.

Adams: Did you tell the lawyer, "I am relieved that I've got somebody here I can talk to. Let me just go on and talk to Detective Ferguson?"

Martin: I did. And he told me not to do that. In fact, I shouldn't have said anything at all to him.

Adams: So while you're relieved that you can finally unload your burden, you don't take the opportunity? Is that what you're telling this jury?

Martin: Yes, sir. I didn't. I did not tell him everything about it. I did not relate everything that led up to it and everything that happened after it.

Adams: Well, excuse me, but the note I made when you were testifying was "I thought I could finally tell someone everything." Isn't that what you testified to, but now you're saying you didn't want to tell him everything?

Martin: In terms of everything, I can say that meaning surrounding the death of my mother, everything about that.

Adams: And the fact that she is concealed for nine days in a home that you're going in and out of on a regular basis does not concern her death?

Martin: No, sir.

Although there are no court notes so stating, it doesn't take much imagination to visualize Adams shaking his head in response to that reply.

Adams: Now you testified that your mother was gagged with a bandanna, and that's the bandanna or scarf that's been admitted into evidence, is it not?

Martin: Yes, sir, it is. It's a pocket square handkerchief that my dad had that I used—after he died—and wore it in a suit coat pocket. It's a paisley print man's pocket handkerchief type article.

Adams: How did it get around your mother's neck?

Martin: It had initially been around her mouth as a gag, and when he took her out of the closet to wrap up the body, he pushed it down over the chin, and it had been knotted tightly around her mouth, and he couldn't undo the knots, and he left it in place. It was loose around her neck.

Adams: You heard the statement from Detective Ferguson? He testified that you said that Larry made you wrap her up and put her in the closet.

Martin: Right. When we wrapped her, I got the blankets for him and the quilt and the other blanket, and he placed her on them, and we wrapped them around (her). Then he wanted to know what we could use to . . . to tie this up with, and I had the (surgical) ties and gave them to him and showed him how to use them. We tied them around (her).

Adams: Well, what were you doing during this period of time while y'all were having this conversation you just related to the jury?

Martin: We were in the house. I was listening to him.

Adams: And going along with his requests?

Martin: Yes, sir.

Adams: The man had just killed your mother, and you just go along with getting him whatever it is that he's asking for?

Martin: I suppose, looking back on it, that I should have allowed Larry to kill me and burn our house down, and that would have been the thing to do. You know, I felt at the time that there would come a time when I could get away from this individual, when I could get out from underneath him and his control, his manipulations, and that I could tell somebody the truth, and that they would believe me. But now I look at it and say, well, they didn't believe me nine days into it. Why would they have believed me twenty-four hours into it or two days into it or whatever?

Adams: When the time came that you could get away from Larry, and you could tell somebody about it, you did not take that opportunity, did you?

Martin: I felt like he could show up at any moment. I didn't know what would happen. He was—after this happened, he was unstable as to when he came and went around me, when I was to speak to him on the phone. As I've already told you, he'd come over at two and three in the morning, things like this. So everything changed.

Adams: The question is that when the time came, and you had an opportunity to get out from under Larry, or get away from him, you didn't take it, did you?

Martin: I did not see it as an opportunity to do that. No, sir, I didn't feel like I had the opportunity to get away from him.

Adams: Well, you heard Officer Thompson

come in here this morning and talk about coming to your house, didn't you? He came out there, and he had a Chatham County Police Car, markings all over it that said, "Chatham County Police," had a light bar on top. He gets out and he's dressed in full uniform. You saw that didn't you?

Martin: Yes, sir, I did.

Adams: And Larry wasn't there, was he?

Martin: No, sir. I'd spoken with Larry on the phone just before the policeman arrived at the house.

Adams: But you didn't tell Officer Thompson, "Look I need some help. I've got a guy that is exerting this unhealthy influence over me, and I need help to get out from under it." You didn't tell him you needed some help, did you?

Martin: No, sir. I told him what I had been told to tell him.

Adams: So we agree that you did not take an opportunity to report the death of your mother?

Martin: Yes, sir.

Adams: Now, when you talked with your Aunt Barbara about the circumstances of your mother's death. Larry wasn't around you, was he?

Martin: No, sir, he wasn't.

Adams: When you called your aunt over at the police department on the following morning, Larry wasn't around, was he?

Martin: No, sir.

Adams: You were in jail, weren't you?

Martin: Yes, sir, I was.

Adams: And you're telling this jury that you didn't tell your aunt, "I killed her?"

Martin: I said Larry did it. I don't know how

it came out, how it sounded. You know I was crying, hysterical, over the telephone when I was talking to her. I never said I did it.

Adams: Why were you crying and hysterical?

Martin: It was a relief to hear her voice, I guess . . . to talk to her.

Adams: Have you not been trained not to display any emotion?

Martin: I've had both sides of it in my family. My dad was a very emotional person, and with him I was allowed to be an emotional person and have feelings. With my mother, that was not an issue; that was something that wasn't encouraged. (My nature) alternates between, I guess, too emotional and not emotional enough. I can't really say (which side I fall on).

Adams: Okay, so when police come and find your mother in the closet, it would not have been unusual for you to exhibit any emotion, would it?

Martin: No, sir.

Adams: But you didn't do that, did you?

Martin: No, sir, I didn't.

Adams: Now, when you knew that the body was being discovered, if you had waited all this time to be able to tell somebody something, why didn't you say something to Sergeant Workman or Detective Hansen?

Martin: I don't know. I really don't have an answer.

Adams: Why, when Detective Hansen and Sergeant Workman gained access to the home, did you turn around and try to walk off?

Martin: I was going to go back to my trailer. That's where I stayed.

Adams: So you're going to let them go in and discover your mother, and you're going to stay in your trailer and still not tell anybody everything about what went on?

Martin: I felt like it was going to happen, that it was fixing to come out.

Adams: Well, weren't you relieved at that point, as you were when you got to see Detective Ferguson?

Martin: Somewhat. I had just smoked some crack prior to the police showing up there, and about an hour or so later, I was in a different state of mind, I guess. I was somewhat nervous and apprehensive (when the police came to the house). I didn't know what the outcome of it would be. I realized that it had gone on for a long time, and I was worried.

Adams: Now you testified that before your father died that you decided you were going to straighten yourself out. How long was that before your father died?

Martin: Approximately two weeks.

Adams: And I believe you said you sat down and talked with your family and sought help in a spiritual way.

Martin: We had prayer. My mother was a minister, and I had been raised in the church and attended church with them until I was probably eighteen or nineteen and started into college.

Adams: Did you ever go to any place and try to address the fact that you were abusing crack cocaine?

Martin: No, sir, I didn't. I wanted to go to Georgia Regional and get help. (But) I felt like there was more to it than just me. I wanted my mother to go with me. I felt like it would be good for both of us, that there were things that emotionally I wanted to come out, that I didn't feel like they could come out, or they hadn't come out.

Adams: The fact is that you never made any attempt to take a constructive step toward getting off crack cocaine, did you?

Martin: Yes, sir. I called Tidelands—not Charter as my aunt testified, because I couldn't afford to go to Charter and didn't have insurance—and made an appointment with them. Initially that was made for depression, but I wanted to talk to them about my other problems. (But) I cancelled the appointment.

Adams: Did you ever call and say, "I've got a drug problem. I need to see somebody?"

Martin: No, sir, I didn't.

Adams: On November 10, you had a conversation with your aunt when your aunt and uncle came to your house. You heard your aunt testify about that today, didn't you?

Martin: Yes, sir.

Adams: Now, you've talked about some checks that you wrote to finance your crack habit, and it was checks on an account your mother was looking after. You, your mother and Mrs. Perry, y'all talked about the fact that you had been forging those checks when your aunt came down in November to talk to you and your mother?

Martin: Yes, sir. It's (the account) called the Women's Temperance Christian Union, WTCU.

Adams: And when you told your aunt out in the yard that you were taking property and selling it, you told her that you were doing that to buy things for Jesse and Larry, did you not?

Martin: Yes, sir.

Adams: Nobody was there but you and your aunt?

Martin: That's right.

Adams: You denied at the time taking drugs, didn't you?

Martin: I denied smoking crack. I told her that I smoked pot.

Adams: Now if you're wanting to get out from under all these things that were leading you astray, why didn't you say something to your aunt at that time?

Martin: I think that the power of the addiction was so strong that there, uh, I was just helpless. I couldn't do anything about really helping myself except just dig myself in deeper.

Adams: As a matter of fact, you have done nothing to try to address the fact that you were strung out on crack cocaine prior to going to jail, have you?

Martin: No, sir.

Adams: (And) if you felt threatened by the way Larry was dealing with you, did you ever ask Jesse to take you to somebody else?

Martin: No, sir. I was afraid that if I told Jesse—he's a very volatile person, very hot-tempered person—I was afraid he would go to Larry and that something might happen to him or, or that it would, it would go bad. So I was actually afraid to tell him.

Adams: Mr. Martin, if you are so afraid of these people that you're spending time with on a continual basis, why didn't you get away from them?

Martin: They were in control. I had no will of my own.

Adams: You do everything that Larry tells you to do?

Martin: I've done everything that everyone's told me to do practically my entire life.

Adams: That's not exactly true, is it, Mr. Martin?

Martin: Well, it began at home with my family, my mother and father, and later it went with teachers and then friends and sexual companions, and mostly lately in the situation with Larry Smith.

Adams: Your mother told you not to be going down to Belk's and taking her credit card and charging eight hundred dollars' worth of jewelry at a time, didn't she?

Martin: Yes, sir, and she cancelled the credit card. Yes, sir.

Adams: You didn't do what your mother said, did you?

Martin: No, sir. There's been conflicts.

Adams: Well, these conflicts usually resolve by doing what Jim Martin wants to do, don't they?

Martin: No, sir.

After verification of Martin's receipt of his revocation of probation:

Adams: You knew that at the time that this spending spree that you'd been on, this life of luxury that you'd been living as relates to buying Larry Smith and Jesse jewelry, fur coats, going and coming pretty much at your leisure, was fixing to come to an end, didn't you?

Martin: Yes, sir.

Adams: And you were going to jail?

Martin: No sir, I didn't know that.

Adams: Well, you read the petition, didn't you? You read that they were trying to revoke your probation, didn't you? And you understand that if your probation was revoked, you were going to wind up in jail, didn't you?

Martin: That's correct.

Adams: The fact remains that on November 21, you knew that shortly the gravy train was going to run dry, didn't you?

Martin: I really didn't have anything left at that point. I was nearing the end of having things to be able to sell.

Adams: It had gotten to a point of where you were going to have to pay the piper, hadn't it?

Martin: Yes, sir.

Adams: And you say you didn't have anything left. Is that your testimony?

Martin: I said I had very little left.

Adams: Well, you still had Jesse, didn't you?

Martin: Yes, sir.

Adams: And that's not anything to you? Did you place a value on your relationship with Jesse?

Martin: Yes, I did.

Adams: You had something else, didn't you, Mr. Martin?

Martin: What was that?

Adams: You still had your mother, didn't you?

Martin: Yes, sir, I did.

Adams: Even after you started forging her name on her Belk's card, your mother tried to protect you, didn't she?

Martin: Yes, sir.

Adams: When you took those checks from the temperance union and you forged your mother's name on it and drew all the money out, your mother tried to protect you, didn't she?

Martin: She did help me.

Adams: And you repaid her by coming in here and telling this jury that your mother has fed you drugs all of your life?

Martin: My mother gave me drugs as a child.

Adams: And you repaid her by putting your hands on that bandanna and strangling her to death on December 10, 1991, didn't you?

Martin: No, sir, I did not.

Adams: And you repaid her when she was laying in that closet, rotting, by calling up places where she was supposed to be and pretending to be her and telling people that she wouldn't be there, that she was sick.

Martin: Larry told me to do that.

Adams: You repaid her by telling your aunt when she called that you missed your mother, and that y'all were all going to get together at Christmas time.

Martin: Yes, sir.

Adams: Do you call that being a dutiful son?

Martin: No sir, not at all. No, sir.

Adams: You have been in jail for thirteen months, your attorney asked you about why you did all these things, and you answered him that you didn't know, that you had thought about it a hundred times. So, by your own testimony, this hasn't concerned you?

Martin: Yes, sir. It has concerned me greatly.

Adams: Concerned you no more than eight times a month, has it?

Martin: That's not true at all. It concerns me every night. I have trouble going to sleep. In fact, since I've been in jail, I've seen four psychiatrists and am now taking medication for sleep and depression.

At that point, letters from the Defendant to Jesse and his Aunt Barbara were brought into exhibit. The letters had no mention of Alva Martin.

Adams: Why not?

Martin: I can't really say. I felt like when I wrote a letter to someone that the main concern of the letter was to address the person and what they might be doing, try to make my situation seem as good as I could make it under the circumstances. I didn't discuss my dad's death, either, and he had just died three months prior to my mother's death.

Adams: The only thing you were concerned about was your cats, isn't that correct?

Martin: My aunt and my grandmother both raise cats, and that's where I get my love of cats from. She's now taking care of both of my cats and has been for over a year.

Adams: You cared enough about your cats to ask your aunt about them when you wrote that letter, didn't you? And you cared enough about your cats to recount the things that you and your cats had done for several years, did you not?

Martin: Yes, sir, I did. It was something that I felt like I could discuss with her without going into something that would be so unpleasant in a letter.

Adams: But you didn't care enough about your mother to even recognize or mention that she was dead.

Martin: That's not true at all.

In redirect by the Defense, Dowell sought to establish that the revocation of probation would not adversely affect the relationship between mother and son, in hopes of persuading the jury that there was no claim of motive there.

Dowell: Did you feel that she'd (Alva) still love you and support you, even after the revocation?

Martin: I knew that she would. Things happened just prior to her death that told me that for sure. Jesse beat me up and broke my glasses, and my mother went out, bought new frames for the glasses for me and paid cash. About two weeks before she died, I hugged her, and she called me "her precious boy."

Dowell: Why did you cancel the Tidelands appointment? Mr. Adams asked you whether you went or not, but he didn't give you a chance to explain.

Martin: I don't know. I was very depressed at the time, and I was strung out on crack. I was afraid of losing my job. My dad evidently knew that he was going to die, and almost on a daily basis, he would discuss the fact that he couldn't live much longer, that he had lived his three score and ten, and he was ready to go, and all this kind of stuff, and it really affected me. And then, when it actually came down to doing it, I don't think I had the courage really to go through with it.

That was the end of Martin's testimony. Dowell attempted to make a demonstration of the difficulty of strangling someone with a bandanna. Its effectiveness was minimal. When the Defense

Attorney said he could twist the bandanna another one hundred eighty degrees, but he would not, the volunteer replied, "I hope not."

At that point, Dowell rested the case for the Defense. Martin said at the time that he was happy with the way Dowell handled the trial.

"He was great. He did everything he could, including really working over (Larry) and pointing out how the detective didn't even follow up on the guy. The detective had decided I was guilty and built his case around that."

In retrospect, years later, Martin would change his mind about Dowell, although he was not bitter. "My problem was that all I knew about the legal system was what I'd seen on *Matlock* and *Perry Mason* on TV."

Adams recalled three rebuttal witnesses, the first of whom was Ralph Allen.

Allen testified that he had never received a foot massage and that he had never been hugged by the Defendant. He maintained that he had never become sexually aroused "as a result of being hugged by the Defendant or any other contact with him." He further stated that he had not ever forced Martin to his knees and had him rub his face against his crotch, nor had he ever forced Martin to "turn away from you, bend over and simulate an act of anal intercourse with him."

Allen further rebutted claims that he and the Defendant had discussed Martin's relationship with Jesse Faucette.

"Have you ever told the Defendant that rather than be with somebody like Jesse Faucette, he ought to find somebody that would buy ice cream for him?" Adams then asked.

"No, sir," Allen replied.

When asked how he felt about Martin's testimony, Allen said, "It upsets me. I've been married for fifteen years, and I have two children. I'm actively involved in the church, in social work like that. I personally take offense to it. I tried to be friendly to Jim. I was curious when he came over, the two times he played the piano, my wife played, we sang church songs. And Jim played some oldie songs and things like that. I was concerned for Jim. I was very fond of Jim's father. I spoke to him every day. I was concerned if Jim knew the Lord as his Savior. I asked him specifically if he did. And here today, to be asked these questions hurts me personally. I've done nothing to cause these allegations to be made against me or about me, and I hate it that I'm here, having to answer and dispute this today."

"Are you concerned," Adams asked in his final question to Allen, "that these allegations might hurt your ministry?"

"I am the minister at a church, a small church here. We're trying our best to build the church the best we very can. I've been pleased to have led one young kid to the Lord this week. I think that that would be devastating that that kind of information be implied against me, and what I can do in my life."

In cross-examination, Dowell suggested that Allen's answers were self-serving.

"So if you admit to what Mr. Martin has implied, it would ruin your ministry, it would ruin your marriage, it would ruin the life as other people know you, is that correct?"

Allen responded, "Sir, the people that know me know I would not do that. I think they would stand beside me. My wife's been beside me for fifteen years. My kids and I . . . . You know, I just hate that it would come to something like this, but my wife would be with me one hundred per cent."

Later, in closing arguments, Ron Adams would ask why Jesse Faucette was not called to the stand to verify Jim's claim that Ralph Allen knew and had met Jesse. Dowell said that it was a point he had not considered, and that all trials have things that might have been done differently, likening the circumstance to "Monday morning quarterbacks" who question a play selection after the game. It's also one of the reasons for the appellate process.

Dowell also pointed out that Faucette had not been very cooperative in pre-trial interviews. "I could have called him as a hostile witness, but the State could have called him and put words in his mouth, and I could not have cross-examined him as my own witness." Another point Dowell made about Faucette: "Would the jury have believed him?"

And there was another point to consider: since Dowell had not talked to Faucette about Allen, he could not be certain that Faucette would not support Allen's claim rather than that of his client.

Barbara Perry was also recalled by the State. Adams' first question was meant to rebut Martin's claim that he had been using prescription drugs, supplied by his mother, for most of his life.

"You testified yesterday that you were familiar with the upbringing of the Defendant. Are you familiar with whether or not the victim in the case was a regular user of the medical profession?" Adams asked.

"Not to my knowledge," Perry replied. "She just didn't believe in doctors. She was a firm believer in taking Vitamin C for everything, and she was very healthy. The only time I remember her being in the hospital was when Jimmy was born, and very few times did I ever know of her going to a doctor. She did go to a dentist a few times."

Adams asked if it would have been against Alva Martin's nature to have made repeated trips to the doctor with her son, and also would it have been against Alva's nature to ply her son with prescription drugs.

Barbara Perry answered "yes" to both questions.

Shifting gears, Adams asked her to recall the phone call she received at the jail.

"He said to me, 'I killed her. Larry made me do it. Larry did it,'" she said.

"And you're sure of that, ma'am?"

"Positive," Barbara Perry replied.

Finally, Adams sought to establish that Martin had never related the same story he told in court to his aunt, even though she had visited her nephew "on a regular basis" after he was arrested.

"During any of these visits, did the Defendant ever mention to you that Larry had a knife or weapon of any kind at any point in time?"

"No."

"Did the Defendant ever tell you that it wasn't he that wrapped up his mother in the blankets, but rather that it was Larry Smith?"

"He told me that Larry made him wrap her in the blankets."

Adams' final question was, "Did he ever tell you anything about her being tied, both hands and feet?"

"No," Barbara Perry replied.

Dowell, on cross-examination, tried to establish that Martin's "I killed her" statement was an emotional rant rather than an accurate report.

"Was he emotional at the time?" Dowell asked.

"Very much so."

"Was he speaking clearly, and could you clearly hear what he said?"

"He sounded as though he was crying. Of course, I was very upset at the time myself."

"But you're absolutely positive of the exact words that you heard?"

"Yes," Barbara Perry answered. "Because I went back in the detective's office and quoted this in front of the detective and my husband."

Finally, Dowell sought to minimize Martin's lack of detail of such things as the knife Larry Smith was alleged to have had.

"As far as the other conversations you had with him at the jail, did he ever go into any great detail at all about the crime with you? Or did he just say that Larry did it?"

"He never went into a lot of detail. He would just give me bits and pieces. And sometimes I would ask him a question, and he would answer me."

"So it's possible," Dowell concluded, "that certain things he left out? That he just didn't automatically tell you the whole narrative?"

"Right," Perry said, ending her testimony.

The final witness was Owen Ferguson, recalled by the State to verify that there had been no mention of Larry Smith's knife in Martin's statements. Ferguson said that there had been no mention of a knife to him.

At that point, both sides rested their cases.

Adams' closing statement was a virtual review of the charges and evidence presented.

Dowell picked at conflicts in Larry Smith's testimony.

"Now he testified that, yes, he helped Jim move certain articles of furniture in and out of the house up until the day of Mrs. Martin's death. But after that, all of a sudden, he never came back in the house and thought it was exceedingly strange that Jim wouldn't let him in the house." He also pointed out that neighbors had seen Smith moving furniture out of the house during the time between Mrs. Martin's death and the discovery of the body by police.

He also argued that Ferguson had not looked into Larry Smith's whereabouts on December 10, that Ferguson had not checked on "anything about Larry," even though Jim had told him, "Larry Smith killed my mother."

"Nothing has been done to eliminate the possibility that Larry Smith killed Mrs. Martin, other than Detective Ferguson accepting Larry Smith's word."

Dowell concluded with a point on addiction.

"Addiction is a very powerful thing," he said. "Crack addition . . . is instantaneous. People get hooked on crack after the first puff. When you combine the awesome addition of the addictive powers of crack with a weak and submissive personality such as Jim Martin's, then you have an extremely powerful weapon that someone like Larry Eugene Smith could use to his advantage."

In rebuttal, Adams countered, "But you will recall that Larry Smith says that he did continue to go over to the house on a regular basis, even during the time Mrs. Martin was missing. Larry Smith told you about the concerns that were raised in his mind because he observed the car sitting in the same place each day."

He also asked some hard questions:

"Why didn't the Defense call Jesse, if he could have taken the stand to corroborate what was said?"

And, Adams asked about Jim Martin: "Why didn't he call (for help) after the murder?

"If, as the Defendant tells you, Larry Smith could make him do anything, why not just have him do it (commit the murder) while Larry Smith is not even in the area?"

Another point, not belabored earlier in the trial, was the bruising on Alva Martin's face.

"If the Defendant was only away from his mother at the time of this killing for one to two minutes, as he testified, then how did he miss the beating? When did the beating occur? What was he doing during the time that the beating was going on? You cannot use his time frame and separate him from what is happening, if you believe the other evidence in this case."

The jury deliberated for only a couple of hours, recessing at 12:51 p.m. for lunch, and reconvening at 2:51 p.m., at which time the foreperson asked for a clarification of the definitions of malice murder, felony murder and voluntary manslaughter. The judge's explanations are listed in Appendix E, found elsewhere in this book.

At 3:58 p.m., the jury returned its unanimous verdict: "We, the jury, find the Defendant, James Mize Martin, guilty of felony murder."

The conviction carried a mandatory life sentence. Court proceedings were ended at 4:02 p.m.

A Life Sentence

"When I heard the verdict, I cried," Barbara Perry said, sobbing as she recalled that day, "because I felt like it was such a waste. That the young man that had all the abilities that he had . . . to spend the rest of his life in prison."

Bill Dowell filed a motion for an appeal, and a hearing was held on August 23, 1993, with Adams again acting on behalf of the State. Brannen again sat at the bench. Willie T. Yancey was Defense Attorney. No trial for appeal ever took place, however. The hearing was held because Dowell had filed for the appeal. Martin had sent two letters to Yancey asking that the appeal not be carried through.

"They put me up for an automatic appeal," Martin said, "and the lawyer they assigned me this time told me, 'Well, we can appeal, but it'll probably be the same thing.' And I do feel a lot of guilt about all that happened. I still do. I feel like I deserve to go the prison. Not for murder, not for life, not for killing her, but if for nothing else than I was an accomplice, whether I was willing or unwilling.

"I was wrong. The whole thing was wrong. I refused the appeal because I felt so much guilt about it. I wrote the judge a letter and told him that nothing that happens now, whether I have an appeal or not, is going to bring my mother back. No amount of talking or anything. And while I didn't kill her, I feel guilt about it, and I guess I feel like I should be punished, which I am."

Jim Martin began serving his life sentence on the night he was arrested for murder. From that night until at least 2006, he has been, and will be, "inside." His only time outside of prison walls has been during his transfers between institutions. And yet, he is surprisingly upbeat.

"If I could sum up my mental attitude in one word, it would be 'positive.' No way would I give in to bitterness, disillusionment or self-pity, or any version of those self-limiting behaviors. It would be a waste of time and energy. I've been trying to make the best of a bad situation. I guess I'm not really frustrated or angry all the time because of the way my life went. I was controlled by my parents and in my sexual relationship. I'm used to being submissive and controlled, and I don't have a problem with that. Authority doesn't bother me. So I think I'm unique compared to a lot of guys in prison who do feel angry or frustrated or resentful."

Although he still maintains that he did not kill his mother—and he has no reason to deny it now that he has served many years for the crime—he says that being sent to prison saved his life . . . that he would have killed himself in pursuit of his drug habit.

"Crack or some combination of getting it and using it would have killed me, yes," he said. "I was down to 140 pounds. Now I weigh 210. . . the most I've ever weighed in my life, and I just hate it." The last comment included a laugh. Since the time of the interview, he tried the Atkins Diet and lost several pounds. But he recently said that he has gained it all back.

He also still does not remember a few things about the night that his mother was murdered. For example, he claims Larry Smith strangled his mother with a necktie, but he says now that he has no idea where Smith got the tie. If Smith had brought it from the camper/trailer, surely he would have noticed that. He also doesn't remember how long he was in his old room while, he claims, Smith killed his mother, or exactly what it was he was looking for when he went to said room. In fact, he suggested that this book might have been titled *Getting Away With Murder*.

His aunt thinks he is truthful in that he does not remember killing his mother or the other details about that night.

"I think he's blacked it out of his mind completely. As far as he is concerned, Alva never existed. There are things you can black out. In the letters Jim writes to me, he never mentions her, never mentions the crime. He sends me Mother's Day cards and tells me I'm the mother he never had.

"When I called one time (after Alva's death but before the discovery of her body), he said, 'Well, mother's going to fix her brownies and her deviled eggs and bring them up.' But she was dead. His saying that is one reason I think he's blacked out some things."

Barbara Perry continued, "I'm not a psychologist, but there are things that I've blacked out in my life and forgotten completely until years and years later, and something would trigger it. I had a recurring dream of being under a house, cemented in, and this would happen night after night for years and years, and all there would be would be a little (slit) where I could see out. Then, all of a sudden, I remembered that when I was just a child, probably five years old, a bunch of teenaged boys dragged me under a house and undressed me. I still don't remember what they did, but I remember getting away, running down the sidewalk, crying, with no clothes on."

Although the evidence against him was overwhelming, Martin claims he did not get a fair trial. While he said immediately after the trial that he thought Bill Dowell did a "great" job, years of reflection have changed his view.

"I think it was a real dumb thing on his part to empanel an all-female jury when the victim was a woman. His logic was that women had more time for this sort of thing, that they were more interested. It was like a soap opera to them, he said, and he said they were traditionally more sympathetic to homosexuals."

Perry was afraid her nephew would have problems in prison. "I always felt like he might have a problem in any prison he went to, because the prisoners are going to take advantage of someone they know is gay and young."

Martin paints a completely different picture.

"I didn't have any expectations or thoughts about it beforehand," he said. "I had heard of stories about abuse by guards and stuff, but I really didn't think that there were going to be a bunch of neo-Nazi guards running around with big German shepherds. And there aren't. It's a very civilized place, in a sense. A world unto itself, obviously."

Hollywood portrays prison frequently as a place where inmates much constantly watch their backs.

"It's not like *Brubaker*, at least not any more," Martin said. "I've never looked over my shoulder. I should, probably, but I don't."

He has never had any significant problems with prison employees. For the most part, he's had few problems with other inmates, although, while at Coffee, he had some issues with other prisoners.

"I just didn't feel comfortable with the population at Coffee. It wasn't the prison, although the staff was kind of green and there was a lot of chaos because of the lack of control. They tried to run everything to precision, even to the point of paranoia. But I guess that since it was private and all, they had to make sure nothing got out of line. The biggest problem at Coffee was the young black boys. They shook their dicks at female officers. I was scared to go out in the yard (common area) because of them. They did a lot of stealing, and I thought they might jump me and rape me. My friends would tell me not to worry, but I couldn't be sure.

"I've been treated *great* by prison employees. Everything here is very clean and sanitary, and I have to say I like the food. Not all of it, but when we have something I really like, like pancakes, I overeat." He stopped and laughed and patted his stomach, then made reference to one of the items available through the prison store. "Of course, the Little Debbies help. You tend to overeat when you do get those things. You'd be surprised how many overweight people there are in prison."

Of course, no prisoner likes everyone who works at prisons. He recalls one warden at Coffee.

"This guy was Deputy Warden of Security, and when he came in to inspect the cells, he would go on and on and talk and talk, trying his best to abuse us verbally and humiliate us," he said. "I prayed about him for the whole time he was there. And before I was transferred, he was let go for sexually harassing one of the female officers."

Martin is thankful for the psychological therapy he has received. He singled out Dr. Carolyn Rasche, who counseled him at Central. "She's in a class by herself. She hypnotized me. I don't remember what all we did, but (if and) when I get out, if I can live in Atlanta (Rasche's practice is in suburban Atlanta), I hope to see her again."

He had praise for others, too.

"The mental health staffs wherever I've been have been the best part of every prison I've been in, and all of them have had really top-notch mental health departments. I can't say enough good things about them. I made a lot of progress because of them. I only wish that during all the things I was going through in my childhood . . . like when I cut my wrists . . . I wish my mother had gotten me therapy then."

Martin says he was ten years old when he made that suicide attempt. It was the only time he tried to take his own life. He displayed his wrists, showing small scars that still remain.

"I think I was just trying to balance too many things at once . . . the model child, the entertainer, the kid running around sneaking off and having sex, the pianist in the church . . . I just couldn't deal with all of it."

Martin also maintains that society's perception of prison being one continuous sodomy camp is vastly out of kilter.

"There's a lot of guys who look at you, and I guess I've been fortunate to have straight friends who look out for me in here," he said. "The black guys drive you nuts sometimes. And I was at a prison in the past that was pretty violent. Every summer there was a black on white riot with about ten white boys taking on forty or fifty blacks. A couple of times, I heard about boys getting raped, but none of that ever happened in my pod."

He was once assigned to what was known as a "predator dorm."

"I saw one black guy beat another one with a lock tied to a sock. There was blood everywhere. And I met a sissy at the same camp whose name was Cornbread. He had been attacked by a gang of young blacks who stuck plastic soft drink bottles up in him. He had to go to the hospital. But after he got out, he was back messing with the black boys again, so I guess some people never learn."

He had a problem with his first roommate when he was transferred to Johnson State Prison in 2004.

"I was laying on my bed on my belly, and all I had on was a pair of Jockey shorts. It was the middle of June and unbelievably hot. I was almost asleep when this young, skinny, ugly black kid—obviously a candidate for compassionate plastic surgery—came into the room. He shut the door, came over to my bed, pulled my shorts down so the cheeks of my ass were exposed, got on top of me and tried to push his penis into me."

Martin said he immediately demanded that the man get away from him.

"He said, 'You know you want it,' and I said, 'No, I don't, get off me.' That went on for ten minutes or so, and he finally got the idea and got up and climbed into his bunk with the parting salvo of 'I'll be jacking.'"

The next day, after some exchanges among Martin, prison officials and the roommate, the man apologized. "He said it wouldn't happen again, but by Thursday night, he was waking me up again, saying stuff like, 'I'm up here jacking.'"

The harassment continued until Martin was afraid he might do something drastic.

"When I'd first reported it, one of the lieutenants said, 'You should have put a lock in a sock and busted him dead in his shit with it.' After a few days, I began having a delayed reaction, and I thought about what the lieutenant had said. He'd called me a killer, even though I'm not one, but the more I thought about it, the more I thought about killing that roommate."

Six days after his initial encounter with the would-be rapist, he signed to go into "protective custody." The following day, he was transferred. "I have a pretty good roommate now," he said.

Most of the sex-in-prison tales, he says, comes from barter-system prostitution.

"Hustlers in here are called fuck-boys, and they are the lowest form of life . . . strictly the bottom feeders in the hierarchy in prison. They get hooked up with usually an older black guy who provides the fuck-boy with dope, cigarettes, coffee or whatever in exchange for fucking his booty.

"The lowest form of fuck-boy will give it up for a cup of coffee or a few cigarettes."

He recalled one story where a young man wanted a pack of cookies. "It was when I was at Columbus. The cookies were about fifty cents then. There were two or three guys involved, and one of them (defecated) and told the fuck-boy if he'd eat some of the shit, they'd give him a pack of cookies. So he did, and the other guys just laughed at him and munched on the cookies while he did it. I think he finally did get two or three cookies out of the pack."

Even though he once told his Nazarene-minister mother, "I hate all you stand for," Martin says he has survived prison because of his only-child upbringing and his faith.

"As an only child, I learned to be content with my own company, and to always have a lot of projects I am interested in. I am never bored. I've read over a thousand books and gotten into my writing.

"Faith is what gets me through, though. It really wasn't a choice for me. Opening myself up and exercising faith in a variety of ways was and is the only way for me. Honestly and truly, I'm more spiritual than I am involved in any religion. I was practicing Buddhism before I got locked up. When I was in Phillips those three years, I attended Catholic services. My uncle was a Catholic. I always thought it was a great religion. Over the years, I've taken bits and pieces of different theologies and ideologies and stitched them together and made myself a sort of spirituality quilt."

He corresponds with his aunt and a couple of friends. His aunt sends him a small amount of money each month. The friends help out less often. He has a job doing proofreading for a friend in the Midwest who operates a mail-order classical record business. The job pays very little, but even a few bucks, he said, can make a dramatic difference. A couple of times he has gotten into debt with prison loan-sharks, who are only too happy to provide a couple of dollars for snacks at usury interest rates.

"I knew better, but I really needed something to pick up me up then, and there aren't many things in here to do that. Sweets are about it."

If he could make one change to the prison system, Martin says he would bring back the program that allowed collegiate study in prison.

"At Phillips, I went through a program sponsored by Mercer University for two and a half years toward a degree in communications. I hope I can still get that degree, and that it won't be outmoded by the time I get out. One of the professors told us that every person who went through the Mercer program and graduated and got out of prison . . . none of them have ever come back to prison. That's a zero rate. That says something. After all, prison is sort of a self-perpetuating industry. We have all these factories at all the state camps, and we have to keep making mattresses and underwear."

Georgia pays its inmates nothing for their work. So Martin has to rely on the money from his proof-reading job, his aunt and his friends if he wants anything beyond the standard prison-issued items.

His favorite jobs in prison have involved working in education with other inmates. In September, 2004, he began working as a teacher's aide in "Literacy" classes at Johnson.

"It's a real joy to be helping the guys with their reading," he said.

His next parole hearing is in 2006. He expects to be discharged.

"I was up for parole in 1998, but nobody gets out in seven years for a life sentence. I've heard of guys getting out after eight or maybe ten years. I don't think there was much review at all the first time. I was told when I was first locked up that I would probably do at least fourteen or fifteen years.

"My counselor at Central told me she thought I'd do fourteen years. Now where she pulled that figure out of the hat, I don't know but she did. And I have a lot of faith and trust in her."

If good behavior counts, Martin says he will be released. At the time this book went to press in May of 2005, his prison disciplinary record was spotless. And, other than in 1991, with his crack-cocaine-inspired crimes of theft and the subsequent murder conviction, he says that his civilian record is clean, too.

"In all my time here, I've not had one disciplinary report. And my life before coming here was not a series of juvenile detentions or anything."

Not even a speeding ticket?

"No, I don't drive. I've never driven a car. I've always been driven. I'm a driven person." He chuckled at the pun. "I'd probably kill myself and a bunch of other people if I tried. I was waiting until I was forty years old . . . that was the year my aunt learned to drive, and she's sort of been my role model. I wanted her to teach me, but, of course, I was in prison when I was forty."

"I think he'll be paroled (in 2006)," Barbara Perry predicted. "But it worries me as to what he's going to do when he gets out. He told me once, 'Now when I get out, I'm going to win the lottery, and I'm going to buy a big house for you and me and Bettie.' I've had people ask me, 'Won't you be afraid of him when he gets out?' But I'm not afraid of him. Unfortunately, however, he can't come and stay here. My husband and his sons won't permit it."

Although she has her reservations about her nephew's potential for success on the outside, her advice to him would be "to try to do something with his life that would be worthwhile."

She remarked, "I've told him all along, since he got to prison, that it was a horrible thing that happened, but that he should turn it around where it can help him and help somebody else."

Perry suggests he would make a credible drug counselor.

"I couldn't go and tell you not to do certain drugs," she said. "I could suggest it, but I've never been there. But a person who has been there can tell you what it does."

Still, she wonders if he will make it if he is released. "I really think the life sentence is too long, but who am I to say? Buddy spent more than half of his life behind bars. He couldn't make it on the outside. He could not adapt. He was happier in jail.

I don't know that Jim would be that way, and I'd hate to think that he'll be locked up the rest of his life."

Although he's not sure what avenue of employment might be open on the outside, Martin is optimistic.

"I've gotten counseling and therapy in here. I still take medication, but I'm healthy for the first time in my life in a way that I've never been healthy before. I realize I'll probably be taking medication for the rest of my life, but that's ok. I think that I could say I would not touch crack again. I know one hit of that is it. I can never have that one hit again."

He also offers a word of advice for those who have not tried crack cocaine: "Never touch it. Never go near it. Stay away from it, whatever you do. It's the worst thing in the world."

Appendix A: Poetry by James Martin

Poetry is one outlet of expression for James Martin. Some of it is tinged with anger, his rage obvious with his mother's treatment of his father and himself. His rage against her piousness and what he perceives, rightly or wrongly, to be her own self-righteousness, comes through many of the lines. His masochistic sexual attitudes, and their kindredness with their sadistic opposites show up in other lines. Some of his poetry has been published; those which have been accepted to publications are noted here as per his own listing. He continues to write poetry as his incarceration continues.

At his request, one submitted poem was withdrawn just before publication. He considers *Death And I* and *I fled* (in both cases, the poems are untitled but the titles listed here are the first lines) to be his two best. *Mere Chere*, he says, was inspired by a recurring dream from the mid-1990's.

How Do You Smell Dysfunction?

Standing on a street corner preaching
   To those who would listen.
Many are called, few chosen:
   A perverse theme
   On a humid afternoon.

He was sprawled against the hood
   Of a 1954 Buick named Genevieve.
Arms folded across his chest:
   Displaying himself like any
   Young, Southern buck.
With that, yeah, I want you;
   Come on over here,
   Look plastered all over his face.

She went on preaching.
In her ankle length grey (sic) skirt,
   White blouse with
   Three-quarter length sleeves.
No jewelry: unless it was
   A thirty-eight year old virgin's
   Cherry slowly turning green.

He did not guess at first meeting —
   Five short months later they would be
   Florida honeymoon bound
With him tied down
   And pussy whipped
   For the rest of his life

Later, only I was told, in appropriately
   About a doctor visit in Florida:

"Your daddy hurt me."
Or the post honeymoon conversation
    With her older sister, where
    She learned for the first time:
    "It's like gold to them."

No wonder my childhood fantasies
    Were of adoption.
More a child of Grandma Blanche,
    Aunt Barbara or half-sister Bettie
    (Lucky child had a different mother)
And, of course, my Daddy.

After Midnight In Savannah *Poetry*

Things I was afraid of at eight:

> That Barnabas Collins truly lived
> In the dark shadowy corners
> Of my room at night
> He would attack me
> Bite my neck
> And drink my blood.
>
> Cousin McAlhaney
> You know the one
> Married to Evenly
> Farther of Curtis
> Stalked me in public
> Restrooms molested me
> In the funeral home
> Uncle Herbert laying there
> And all the family gathered round
> Wailing making photos
> Of the corpse climbing
> Into the casket.
>
> That I would die young
> Like a twelve year old girl
> Small still waxy
> Brain tumor in
> Permanent remission
> Same antebellum
> Funeral home mansion
>
> That the round
> Twisted shapes
> Of my bed clothes

Housed snakes
Lying in wait
To strike.
If I lay real still
Without moving a muscle
I might be spared

After Midnight In Savannah

I fled
Through chests of drawers
Along a barely delineated path
Of old costumes and props
Discarded years ago.
Surely, this was a short-cut
Designed to lead to him.
Even so, those two girls
Rehearsing their play told on me.
But no one came after
From the backstage world
Of my subconscious vision.
Landing in a big claustrophobic room
Suddenly with two inexplicable puppies in tow
Confronted at once by a woman
Holding forth on the second coming of Christ.
Droning on about a ray from the heavens
And how the world would shatter
Like a sheet of glass, I asked
"What about these puppies?"
"They will perish, too, even though
The truth is in their bodies."
Was her response.
I fled
Into a bath with humid rooms
Opening one into another.
Surely here, in the world of half-naked men
Sharing secrets; in beds side by side,
I would find him.
Some of them I recognized
Running around thumping them with my towel.
But the one I sought
Could not be found among them.

Mere Chere

It was a gray day,
The ninth anniversary.
Would it rain and obscure the pain,
Or snow and cover all below:
Certainly remembering
Would pierce the clouds,
Burst upon the mind
As fireworks backlight
The Eiffel Tower
On Bastille Day.
A day the gates swing open
And prisoners flee
In some jubilation.
The clatter of sabots
On cobblestones.
Outward sights and sounds
Of free men masked
Against inner torment.
A landscape of recurring dreams —
Nightly dramas unfold
With pulse quickening familiarity.
We are standing side by side
Seeking our reflections in
A black draped oval mirror:
Even insignificant objects
Simulate mourning.
Electric storm outside
Lightning flashes
Giving intermittent illumination
But no matter how strongly
I feel her presence

After Midnight In Savannah   *Poetry*

My face is the only one
Looking back.

— Accepted for publication by *Dream International Quarterly*

After Midnight In Savannah

Daddy's side thought too much with their sex.
Fought with desire like gladiators with christians.
Tried a half-hearted, white-wash job over lust
That burned through every time
With a heat so hot, it blistered
Every place it touched
Mother's side lived
On the placid surface of perfection
In perpetual pretense that sex did not exist
Except as whispered secrets behind locked doors
All duty no pleasure like supplicating missionaries
Courting storks in cabbage patches for babies.
But not me precious, I'm your baby, fuck off.
As a seven year old sexual wonder kind
Prowling in predatory fashion preying
On furtive strangers in public places.
Flying in the face of perdition.
Busy accepting my becoming.

After Midnight In Savannah

Death and I are old friends
Eyes looking over my shoulder
Toward a land unseen by me
Friends and acquaintances
Dropping like flies
Black painted glass paned carriages
Black bays tossing blacked plummed (sic) heads
Snorting like the hounds of hell
Have ridden to a final resting place
The pall has been borne
Until ebony boxes blur
One into another
Sounds of hooves clopping
Rhythm of dirt clods falling
Was it any wonder
I found myself in Laurel Grove
A gilded world of familiar dead
Just before dusk light fading
Edges blurring sepia tinted
Faces from old photographs
Rustle of funereal veils
Or limbs of centuries old oaks
Rubbing their Spanish moss
Draperies in damp atmosphere
Antebellum memories shimmering exclusively
Heavens mistially weeping
Tears were falling
From ruined eyes of marble angels
Stained by marks of old downpours
Bent in gently guarding eternal rest

W.W.S.D.

She went to sleep and woke
In God's new heaven.
Now, only she knows where Jesus is;
Since she now sits at the right hand
Of God the Father.
It must be tougher than ever
To get into heaven these days.
No make-up, jewelry or sex.
Her only problem was probably
With certain former sinners,
Already there when she arrived.
After all, she had not been
Responsible for their salvation.
So surely they were suspect.
No Catholics, Buddhists or Muslims.
For all we know
There is a war in heaven
This minute the streets of gold
May be littered with those
Whose heavenly bodies failed
Beneath the all seeing eye
Of her perfection.
But for those happily left behind;
Let us thank what ever our Gods may be,
And cremation, she's gone.

Tin Cora Boom

All that's left is rag and bone
Parade for rest, it never came.
Fraulin (sic) Elizabeth's war torn/time romance
Good German people (not Nazis)
An open-armed welcome with schnapps
Let me call you Schatzi, sweetheart.
Meanwhile, back on Tybee Island...
The moon was a silver dollar
Hanging over a beach cottage w/palms
Where babies slept alone
Betsy smoking, drinking; waiting tables
Found her war work screwing
Lonely soldier boys on leave.
Later, my mother, Alva,
Who Daddy nicknamed Hitler,
Tried to banish every trace:
Burned letters of names verboten.
    But love can live as ashes
    In grey (sic) shadows on a face
    Whisper over Death's rattle
    Burn in a heart forever
    Finally find a hiding place.

After Midnight In Savannah

I once saw Murrieta striding
Through a field of wind tossed poppies:
Their unique red faces upturned,
As if expecting an important word
From the hero of the revolution.
Then, I thought of all the martyr's blood:
A different red from these flowers;
Out my windows, wind whipped
In sudden gusts of ecstasy,
As puffs of pollen escaped riotously.
I found myself holding my breath,
Which slipped from my lips like a sigh.
At last, I heard the music.
Piano, then the melancholy voice
Of Koshetz singing the songs
Rechmaninov taught her:
> In the silence of the mysterious night.
> Do not sing, my beauty.
> Again, as before, I am alone.

— Accepted for publication by *The Raven Chronicles*

I'm Ready

I like to be taken down
From those white columns
Oh I do like to be taken off
Of those white columns
And be made to feel
What one of them
White trash trailer park girls
In a peroxide memory feels
When there has been
Enough beer
Enough heat lightening (sic)
And enough rain
To wash away
Everything that is not real
That is not sweaty
That is not smelly
That does not taste
Like some part of the earth
My senses come alive
My fences become invisible
And there is no
Tangible barrier between
You and me and desire.

— Accepted for publication by *Poetry Motel*

After Midnight In Savannah

Don't want to live without your sex
Can't survive without our lust:
Blinding heat draws us forward,
Licked by flames of undoing.
Too many restraints.
Too many complaints.
Sing a song of six pences, pockets full of wry
Fortune in my man's eyes; torn from cookies
Leaving crumbs behind a sly wall of Chinese desire.
Among the tall trees, swaying branches
Seem to say: come satisfy me.
Damn the consequences.
Damn the torpedoes.
Hidden threat in a pair of pants.
Wanna wanna get me one of those fine guns:
Blast that powder cap against the back of my skull

— Accepted for publication by *Black Roses*

After Midnight In Savannah

Ever get that urge again
For unspeakable
Un reachable (sic)
Unipeachible (sic) place
You inhibit inhabit
Way down yonder
In chronic town
Little turd
Little bird
With your
Cheesy surreality
Your zest for death
Better have a test
Find a way
Pay to play
Stop those alto flashbacks
Black bucks
Fucking you up
Chuck buster
Nut tutu many times
That showgirl said it all
"You're a whore darlin'."

— Accepted for publication by *Black Roses*

Appendix B:
A sermon from Alva Martin

This sermon, entitled *A Recipe for a Happy and Contented Life for 1990* was delivered by Rev. Alva Martin on January 28, 1990:

(End of hymn)

You really didn't know it, but that was one of my husband's favorite songs. I want to say here, too, friends, that I appreciate the wonderful, sweet Christmas card that you sent me with all those signatures on it. That was just tremendous. I think I'll keep that as long as I live. I'll have a special place for that. It was real sweet of you to do that. I'm sure from eating all of your nice goodies here when you had your dinners, that you ladies use quite a few recipes in your cooking, those nice cakes and pies and other things that you prepare for yourselves day by day, and for us, too. And I'm calling this little message, "A recipe for a happy and contented life for 1990." That's what I want you to have, friends. I want you to have a happy and contented life.

This scripture portion here is the recipe, and I want you to listen what it contains. It's very, very important. Now it's good for us to have a good recipe for us to bake something here for our physical bodies. But this is a far more important recipe, because this is for our spiritual needs. First, we're

After Midnight In Savannah   *Sermon*

going to start here in Philippians, chapter four, beginning with verse four. It says, "Rejoice in the Lord, always, and again I say, rejoice." God wants us to rejoice and to praise him for the things that he does for us from day to day. And that's the first ingredient that I'm using here is *rejoice*.

Then it says here, "Let your moderation be known unto all men, the Lord is at hand." So the second ingredient for happiness and for a contented life is to *be careful for nothing*. That means do not be overanxious for anything. I know sometimes I have to tell myself that, because I do get too anxious a lot of time for things. I like to see things happen, and I like to try to help them happen, if I can. And maybe sometimes I get a little too much. But nevertheless, God doesn't want us to be overanxious for anything. Be careful for nothing.

But here's what he does want, and this is a very important ingredient in this recipe: *prayer*. By prayer and supplication with thanksgiving, let your requests be made known unto God. All on Earth can pray. Pray in your own way. God hears and answers prayer, and He invites us to come to his throne, in fact, boldly, and pray. So that's an important recipe for happiness.

Part of our recipe (is) *the peace of God*, which passes all understanding, shall keep your hearts and minds through Christ Jesus. The peace of God. Oh, how we need the peace of God. How the world needs peace today. Just peace in the world would be something wonderful. But the peace of God passes all understanding. We cannot understand the mighty things of God. But that's what keeps us. It keeps our hearts and minds through Christ Jesus.

After Midnight In Savannah Sermon

It's one thing to come to Christ and confess our sins and repent and let Christ come into our heart, but it's quite another thing to walk with Jesus day by day and allow him to keep us . . . and he will keep us if we put our trust in him, our hand in his hand, and he will walk with you every step of the way during 1990 if you will allow him to.   We don't know the things that are going to confront us . . . of course not . . . but we do know one who does know because he says he has gone the way before us, and he knows the way that we came. We have Jesus Christ. All our lives, the peace of God will keep our hearts.

Now here's something that's going to help us to have this peace that I was talking about there. And that's what we think about. In this eighth verse, it says, "Finally, reverend, whatsoever things are true, whatsoever things are honest, whatsoever things are just, whatsoever things are pure, whatsoever things are lovely, whatsoever things are of good report, if there be any virtue, and if there be any praise, think of these things." Think of these things. God tells us what to keep our minds stayed on. You know, if people would get their minds—I'm talking about generally speaking now in the world—off of themselves and off of things and off of trying to do things and get their minds on these things that God told us to think about, then that's their pathway to peace, and they will harvest peace if they can keep their minds on these things. Notice here in the ninth verse, "Those things,"—this is Paul talking to the church there at Phillippi—"those things which ye have both learned and received and heard and seen in me, do."   And then it says "The God of peace shall be with you." Then we have to do those things. It's one thing to hear it. It's one thing to go out and be present. But it's another thing to do those things that you've heard. . . do those things that the Bible tells us to do. Be ye doers of the word and not hearest always, the Bible says. So Jesus wants us to do these things. Keep your mind on the good things. Don't allow the Devil to put anything in your mind that wouldn't make you feel good and comfortable. If you start thinking about something that you think you're going to get discouraged, just get it out of the way and start thinking on these things that God told us to think about and, friends, you're going to be happier. You're going to be more contented as you travel down the road of this new year.

Now there are some particular things here that I read to you here in the scripture. First I want to mention where it says "be careful for nothing." In other words, that means "do not worry." Do not worry. Do not worry about anything. I know sometimes it isn't easy, but we can by the grace of God, we don't have to worry. Did you know that worry will burden you down? Worry burdens us down. We don't have to be burdened down with worry. Worry really can, literally, destroy us, friends, because it affects our physical life, it affects our heart, it also causes stomach problems if you worry. Why do I say that? Because when we eat our food, if we're worried and excited, it doesn't digest like it should and it will cause eventually stomach problems if we continue to be that way. And God wants us to be as healthy as we possibly can. The Bible says with his stripes we were healed.

After Midnight In Savannah Sermon

He went to the cross for our physical body as well as our soul. Of course we know the soul is more important than the body, that's true, but God would prefer that we would feel good and be well and be happy. And so we need not worry, because it brings on not only what I have mentioned but many other diseases can be traced back to a worried life. I know high blood pressure can. Because that's one thing that causes it, is a lot of worry and tenseness that causes it, so let's try not to worry. You know, friends, we worry about many things that absolutely never happen. Sometimes just silly little things that do not happen. We do not gain a thing when we worry. Really, we lose. We're on the losing side when we allow the Devil to cause us to worry.

I want to read a portion of scripture here to base what I just said. We're going to turn over here to Luke, chapter ten, and I want to read about two good friends of Jesus, Mary and Martha. You have read about them before and you have heard that they were sisters of Lazarus who he (Jesus) brought forth from the grave. But let's notice in the thirty-eighth verse, "Now it came to pass, as they went, that he entered into a certain village, and a certain woman named Martha received him into her house. And she had a sister called Mary, which also sat at Jesus' feet and heard his word. But Martha was cumbered about with much serving and came to him and said, "Lord, dost thou not care that my sister has left me to serve alone? Bid her therefore that she help me." Now I know that I've been heard in my kitchen. And I've been cumbered about with much serving, you might say, on occasion, because when my son comes home from work, well, he

After Midnight In Savannah   Sermon

wants his supper yesterday. Well, really, he wants it ready when he comes in the door. And I'm over there hurrying around, trying to get everything on the table and trying to make it be as nice as I can, really. I don't always succeed, but I try. But here she (Martha) was. No doubt, she might have dropped a lid—a pot lid. "Oh my goodness, why did that have to happen? The Lord evidently heard that noise." And she might have stood over here and started to stir up something and maybe some of it fell on the floor, and she said, "I've got to get that up before he comes in here." She was cumbered about with much serving. Now the Bible doesn't say that happened, but it could have. Because I know it happens to me sometimes. And it does to you, too. So here she was, all upset and excited about what she was preparing for the Master. Well it was all right to fix him a nice meal, of course, but she was taking too much care with it. She wanted every little thing to be just so. And here's what Jesus said to her: "Martha, Martha, thou art careful, and troubled about many things. But one thing is needful, and Mary has chosen that good part which shall not be taken away from her." Of course, we're applying this spiritually now. Of course, we are supposed to, spiritually speaking, sit at the Master's feet and not allow the devil to let us get way off into something that wouldn't be good for us to be into. That's another meaning of that portion of scripture there. But the main thing that Jesus is bringing out is that he doesn't want us to be too taken up with things that would cause us to get worried and frustrated and lose sight of the best things. See, I think that's what he's telling us here in this about not worrying.

All right, the second thing that I want to mention here is (to) pray. We read it here in the scripture, and I didn't say a word about it. But friends, we need to pray about everything. I don't know if you find yourself praying about everything, but I do . . . even little things like fixing a faucet that my husband's trying to fix, or a part of a fixture in the bathroom. I prayed real hard, I said, "Lord, help him." Now my husband . . . in his work. he was very efficient, but he is not really a plumber. But he does do good, though, however, but I asked God to help him. And not let him get nervous about it. Because sometimes you menfolk know if you start to do something, it'll do just like us ladies when we start to do something sometimes. So I prayed, and God, He gives happiness, so He was going to get it fixed. But I just mentioned that to say if you say, "Should you pray about that?" Sure. Pray about anything that comes into your life. That's why I mentioned that. It's just to say that everything is important to God that we have to endure in this world. If it concerns you, he's concerned. And we need water; all of us do. We need to use the parts of our homes as long as we live in them, and God knows that, and He's going to help us with those things.

All right, we pray about everything. Realize your dependence upon God. *Realize your dependence upon God.* I'm afraid sometimes all of us try to do things by ourselves, and we don't take time to ask God to help us. I'm afraid we do. James over there said this, "Ye have not because ye ask not." And God wants us to ask. He's interested in you, friends. Even to the minute details of your lives. He loves everything about you. You're special, as you've heard me say, many times, to God, but it's true, it's so very true. He's the way maker. As I said a minute ago, he will make a way for us. He is concerned about everything that concerns you and me. I don't know the way to take sometimes. Sometimes it just seems like I don't know which way to go. I don't know which path would be better to follow. So I have to get down on my knees and say, "Lord, show me here what you want me to do. Show me the way that I'm supposed to go in this situation or whatever." And God will show you the way.

And then we said over here we need to be thankful. Be thankful in everything. I don't know if you listened to the Atlanta minister the other evening on the TV, but I did, and it said, "in everything give thanks" was his subject. And he asked those people: "You say I'm supposed to give thanks when I'm not feeling good? I'm supposed to give thanks when things are not going my way? How in the world am I going to do that?" Sure, we are. And one reason that he gave was this: he said when we begin to give thanks to God... when we're ill or something is terribly wrong, we're having a very serious problem . . . it's because it helps us to understand the purpose. There is a purpose, there is a reason for everything that happens in your life and in my life. And if we start praising the Lord and thanking him, it helps us to understand, and it helps us to be able to bear it. Be thankful for what you do have. You know you can say, "Well, I don't have this, and I don't have that, and I wish I could do this," but just start praising God for what you do have and see how much that He will bless you. Because, let me say this, things could be a lot worse. Things could be a lot worse in our lives. And if we start praising God for what we do have. I know my husband and I both have said this around the house: "Oh I just have so much to do." And the other day, I said, "Well, let's just thank God that we're able to do it." And he said, "That's right. Let's just thank God that we're able to do it." Even though we do have a lot to do. So let's thank God, whatever happens. The song says, "He will carry you through; he will carry you through; trust in the Savior and be true. For trials come and they will, Jesus will carry you through."

Now the last thing that I want, it says think the right thing, and we mentioned several things here in the scripture that he told us to think, a list of things. You know the words: let's be positive thinkers . . . think positively and not negatively. Now you've heard people who're negative thinkers. You can tell them maybe that you don't feel well, and first thing you know, they'll have you in the hospital. And then maybe you can say, "Well, I'm not feeling all that good," and somebody says, "Well, we'll pray and maybe you'll feel better." In other words, have a positive outlook about it. Try to think positive in what you're thinking, and that'll help you. It really will. I've tried it and I know. Now the Bible says this: "As a man thinketh in his heart, so is he." We know that the mind greatly controls the body; you know that without me mentioning it here. The mind does greatly control the body. Let somebody have a stroke or something happen to their brain, and they cannot use portions

After Midnight In Savannah   *Sermon*

of their body. That's proof right there that the mind greatly controls the body. But it does. Now the Devil wants to destroy it. He wants to destroy your peace of mind, yes he does. He doesn't want you to be happy in 1990. He doesn't want you to be contented, he wants you to be frustrated, he wants you to be worried, so he can get control of your life. But God wants to give you that peace of mind. And if we obey God's word, if we trust in Him completely, his peace will keep our hearts, his peace will keep our minds, his peace will flood our souls, Sister Johnson. And we can look up and say, "Praise the Lord, whatever comes our way."

    God is always there, he always will be there, he always has been, there will never be a time when God will not be. So let's keep our eyes on Jesus, and like the psalm that says, "I will lift up my eyes to the hills from which cometh by him," let's do that for this new year. Let's pray. Let's think good thoughts. Let's not worry, what do you say?

      God bless you good, you listened good today. We've enjoyed being with you.

After Midnight In Savannah *Sermon*

Appendix C: Family Photographs

Jim Martin, Age 2½

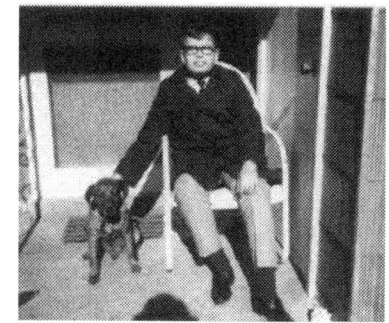

Age 8

Age 9

From a "photo booth"

Playing in snow, a rarity in Savannah

Jim, Age Unknown

After Midnight In Savannah   *Family photographs*

Jim with father Emerson Martin

Siblings Bettie & Buddy

Alva, Emerson, Barbara Perry, Jim

Emerson-Alva Wedding

Alva at a young age

Alva in the 1980's

Alva in 1990

After Midnight In Savannah *Family photographs*

Emerson & Alva Martin

Alva Martin, Christmas 1985

Jim & Emerson, Christmas 1985 (left) and 1986 (right)

Emerson & Alva, Christmas '86

Tombstones, Emerson & Alva

Appendix D: "Don't Go There"

(This is an essay written by Jim Martin for students at the request of his aunt, Barbara Perry).

You hear it all the time. Someone will say, "Don't go there." And, the other person will say something, and the first person will say, "You had to go there." But believe me, where I am: you do not want to go there.

Where am I? I am in prison doing a life sentence. I've been here over 10 years now, and maybe I'll get out in 2006. 15 years out of my life. Who would want to lose 15 years out of their life, or maybe even more? And, yet, I live everyday with many other men who have been here that long or longer. Some have children who have grown up without them and now are strangers to their fathers. They may lose a father, mother, sister, brother while they're here. Most are not even allowed to go to the funeral.

Sound like the kind of life anyone would want? One of the easiest things to say is, "Well, that'll never happen to me." Keep on kidding yourself. Keep on giving yourself enough rope, and eventually you will find yourself hung out to dry here.

It's the little things that add up. The little things you tell yourself, "Oh, this won't matter, this is nothing." But all those nothings become something over time, and before you know what's happening, you've lost control of your life. And there's always someone eager to take control for you. So don't let a person, a situation or anything take control of your life from you.

You know, older folks always say youth is wasted on the young. Whatever you do, don't let it be wasted on you. You are right now at the beginning of your life as a grown person. And there is nothing, nothing at all, that you can't make happen for yourself. Don't let yourself settle for second best. Don't tell yourself, "I could never do that," because whatever your dream for your future is, you can make it a reality. Remember, a journey of a thousand miles begins with one step.

So take control of your life, and make all the good things happen. Sure it will take time. And the lure of easy money is a strong one. But there are no shortcuts. There is no easy money. Whatever you get has to be paid for. Please don't pay for it with years out of your life in a place like this. What you lose in prison can never be got (sic) back, can never be made up for.

I wish for each and every one of you the courage to stand tall on your own two feet and take control. Keep your eyes on the prize and keep reaching for the stars. And, whatever you do, don't come here, don't be trapped in this dead-end world where no one is going anywhere.

Appendix E: Explanation Of Murder Charges

At one point in deliberation, the jury in the trial of James Mize Martin requested an explanation between malice murder, felony murder and voluntary manslaughter. The judge explained the differences as follows:

A person commits **malice murder** when that person unlawfully and with malice aforethought, either express or implied, causes the death of another human being. Express malice is that deliberate intention unlawfully to take away the life of another human being, which is shown by external circumstances capable of proof. Malice may but need not be implied where no considerable provocation appears and where all of the circumstances of the killing show an abandoned or maligned heart. It is for the jury to decide whether or not the facts and circumstances of this case show malice. Legal malice is not necessarily ill will or hatred, but it is unlawful intention to kill, with justification, excuse or mitigation.

A **felony murder** involves a killing that takes place and grows out of the commission of a felony, and it is defined as follows: A person commits the crime of felony murder when in the commission of a felony that person causes the death of another human being, irrespective of malice. Under our law, aggravated assault is a felony. And I had described an aggravated assault to you before as an assault with the intent to murder, rape, or rob, or with a deadly weapon, or any object, device, or instrument which when used offensively against a person is likely to or actually does result in serious bodily injury. And I charged you that an instrument may be shown to be a weapon likely to produce death by direct proof to the character of the weapon, by an exhibition of it to the jury, by evidence as to the nature of the wound, or other evidence which would justify the jury in finding that the instrument was one likely to produce death. The State has alleged that the deadly weapon was in fact a bandanna or a scarf.

A person commits **voluntary manslaughter** when that person causes the death of another human being under circumstances which would otherwise be murder, if that person acts as a result of a sudden, violent or irresistible passion, resulting from serious provocation sufficient to excite such passion in a reasonable person.

If there should have been an interval betwen the provocation and the killing sufficient for the voice of reason and humanity to be heard, which the jury in all cases shall decide, the killing shall be attributed to deliberate revenge and be punished as for murder.

Appendix F:
A drive through Bona Bella

While doing research in Savannah a couple of years ago, the author drove through the neighborhood in which the Martin family lived. That neighborhood, known as Bona Bella, is not an impoverished area, but it's far from the glamorous Historic District for which Savannah is known. The following is a transcript of an audiotape made during that drive down Livingston Avenue:

The neighborhood does not seem to be well kept. A mailbox is rusted out, one yard is grown high, next to it is a well manicured yard with a reasonably well kept garden (although there are a lot of bare spots in it). Foliage grows along the street.

And now I am coming up on the old Martin house, and it has a red brick-appearing front with a bicycle parked in the front of it. Relatively new tile roof, obviously shingles on the side, red shingles, central air unit which looks fairly new on the right side of the house, a lawn chair in the front yard along with a meat smoker and some picnic type furniture, the lawn's been cut but obviously not had any work done on it, no car in the driveway.

Across the street, there is a house with an undone lawn, a pickup truck which may or may not be

After Midnight In Savannah Bona Bella

operational, a number of rugs or rags of some sort thrown over a fence (being dried?). Palm fronds grow wild (or maybe not wild) along the street. The next block which is pretty much more of the same, a sign in front of the house was originally for sale by owner, now for rent by owner. A man in a wheelchair, a house that needs paint very badly, two relatively nice looking brick ranch homes on one side and another across the street. At the very end of the street, it dead ends into to the Bona Bella Marina and Bar, which has a sign boasting live bait, shrimp, dockage and ice, with a blue silhouette of a fish not looking too happy.

Where the street ends, there is no civilization beyond the marina/bar, only grasslands and forests. It appears to be forests on the back sides of the neighborhood; at least it is heavily treed.

Livingston Avenue is narrow, no lines, 25 mph speed zone, "Slow Children" sign with the silhouette of a child running; one house has a basketball goal, another has a boat on wheels with a Suzuki motor and a plastic bucket holding up its front end. Another house has unusual shades that are partially drawn, partially rolled up. Another house has a white Chevette in front of it. The house appears to be in renovation. Another yard has a sign that says, "Beware of dog," with a pile of scrap metal out in front of the house. Another has plastic sheeting covering its roof; it doesn't appear to be occupied.

One street sign mistakenly reads "Livingstone

Avenue." No recent or new cars; most of the neighborhood is old, not saying it's the poor side of town but certainly not the Ritz. A sign urges voters to choose its candidate in an upcoming school board election.

One additional note: Livingston Avenue is just outside the border of the city limits of Savannah, according to the map of the city purchased at a local convenience store. The Herb River runs nearby.

Appendix G: Miscellaneous Notes

Among the things found in researching Alva Martin's murder:

Witnesses for the Defense were listed as: Barbara Perry, Jesse Thomas Faucette III, Larri Smith, Marion Cooper.

Alva Martin's death certificate listed her as 5 feet 7 inches tall and weighing 149 pounds.

Items Alva Martin was wearing when she was killed, as received from Dr. Sperry after the autopsy: one rust colored jacket, one plaid skirt, one white bra, one pair of white underwear, one print blouse.

Detective Ferguson's notes:
On 12/20/91 at 0010 hours, I advised James Martin of his Constitutional Rights and he signed the rights form. Martin had previously signed the Search by Permission forms for both the house and small camper trailer in the back yard (Search Warrant was obtained).

Once I advised James Martin of his Constitutional Rights, I advised him I wanted to talk to him about his mother. He gave me a slight remark and said yes we need to talk about that. I then asked him why did he kill his mother? He without any emotions or sympathetic thoughts stated, why I didn't do it, Larry did it. He claimed Larry Smith, black, male killed his mother on 12/10/91 by using a necktie around her neck. He claimed Larry made him wrap her up in the blankets and tie her up like a pig and hide her in the hall closet. He also was made to steal from her and sell the property for cocaine. He misused his mother's credit cards and sold her TV to a pawn shop. I then advised James I wanted to tape the interview and he them (sic) stated he wanted a lawyer. I did not question him any further. I advised James he was under arrest for Murder, and his only response was he wanted a cigarette.

Suspect information: James Mize Martin, 35 y.o.a., DOB 7/31/56. (Address and SSN were also listed but are not being published here).

I did allow Mr. Martin to contact Attorney Mark Becton at home (phone number listed but not published here). Mr. Becton advised him not to talk about the murder.

The sentencing document listed Jim Martin as follows: Race W, Sex M, DOB 7/31/56, SSN (listed, not published here), Eyes blue, Hair brown, Height 6'1", Weight 150, POB Georgia, Distinguishing marks and scars: scar over right eye, Marital status single, Occupation unemployed, N/A for name, address and relation of nearest relative or friend.

Before the hearing, the Defense filed a *Motion In Limine* to prevent the Prosecution from introducing certain evidence. Among the things listed in that motion:

"To refrain absolutely from making any mention or reference to the specified evidence or testimony on the following grounds:
1. According to the above-styled indictment, the trial will involve a determination of guilt or innocence of the Defendant on the charge of Possession of Controlled Substance.
2. This Defendant believes and hence alleges that at his trial the State will attempt to introduce a statement made by the deceased victim to the effect that the Defendant had choked her with a necktie on a previous occasion. This statement was allegedly made in the Defendant's presence. This will introduce inadmissible hearsay evidence which bring the Defendant's character into evidence in violation of his constitutional rights.
3. On 12/10/91, the victim was killed. The statement by the victim which the State is attempting to introduce was made on 10/15/91. The hearsay exception under which the State will be attempting to introduce the statement is the presence of the Defendant when the statement was made. For the reasons stated in the Defendant's brief, this statement would amount to impermissible hearsay evidence and should not be presented to the jury.
4. This Defendant has been informed by the

State that the prosecution will attempt to introduce evidence of Defendant's previous conviction and subsequent probation for theft charges as well as pending charges against the Defendant for illegal use of the victim's credit cards.
5. This Defendant is accused of strangling the victim with a necktie. The similar transaction which the State is attempting to introduce before the jury is a probation revocation hearing on a misdemeanor theft charge, a theft which did not involve the victim, as well as pending charges involving the use of the victim's credit cards. Neither of these prior acts are similar in nature to the charge of murder under which the Defendant is being prosecuted.
6. The Defendant's right to a fair trial will be compromised if the State is allowed to introduce any evidence of the statement made by the deceased victim as well as any evidence of the Defendant's probation revocation and the pending charges against him for illegal use of credit cards.
7. It is immaterial and unnecessary to the disposition of this case and contrary to the rules of evidence recognized by law in this state to permit such evidence or inference and would be highly prejudicial to this Defendant in the minds of the jury in that an introduction of such evidence would create in the minds of the jury an unfounded presumption of guilt and

would place Defendant's character at issue.

8. An ordinary objection during the course of the trial, even if sustained with proper instructions to the jury, will not remove the effect of such evidence from the minds of the jurors. An instruction by the Court to disregard this evidence would not cure the effect that this impermissible evidence would have on the average juror; therefore, this timely motion is made prior to trial so that no prejudice will result from the use of the objected-to evidence.

Wherefore, it is respectively requested that this Court issue an order prohibiting the State, including the District Attorney, agents of the State, and any and all witnesses to be called in the trial of this case, to refrain absolutely from making any mention or reference, either direct or indirect, regarding the above-described statement by the victim, and the prior conviction of the Defendant on theft charges and pending charges of illegal use of the credit cards.

Respectfully submitted this 29th day of January, 1993, William A. Dowell.

Acknowledgements

I have many people to thank for their help with this book.

** Thanks to the staff in the Chatham County Courthouse for their help in getting me the records from this case. It was my good luck that I happened to meet Brenda Kennedy, who had been on duty at the trial of Jim Martin in 1993, while doing the research at the courthouse.

** Thanks to the Georgia Department of Corrections and especially the staff at Coffee Correctional Institute in Nicholls, Georgia, for their outstanding cooperation in allowing me to interview Jim Martin.

** Thanks to Julia C. Muller for her help in researching the stories of the case in the *Savannah Morning News* and *Savannah Evening Press*.

** Thanks to all those involved who spoke with me, including Bill Dowell, Owen Ferguson and Brenda Kennedy.

** Thanks to James Mize Martin for his candor, his cooperation and for his poetry. He said that my visit to Coffee Correctional to interview him was the only visitation he had received since 1993, when he was transferred from Chatham County to the state prison system. As this book goes to press in May of 2005, he has yet to receive another visitor.

** Thanks to Barbara Perry, whose insight, candor and comments tied this story together in a way that it otherwise could never have been done. I also thank Mrs. Perry for the family photos, for the tape of Alva Martin's sermon, and for the correspondence she gave me from the days of the courtship of Emerson and Alva.

When I first contacted Mrs. Perry for an interview, she agreed, saying she wanted "the truth to come out." I thought that perhaps she would support her nephew's theory that he had not killed Alva. That idea was dispelled in a hurry. The first thing she said was, "I think he did it." Then she explained the story of the family.

Larry Smith's name was spelled three different ways in different court documents. In addition to the standard "Larry," it also appeared as "Larri" and "Larrie." In the interest of consistency, I have used the common "Larry" spelling throughout this book. Attempts to locate him were unsuccessful. Alas, Larry Eugene Smith is a rather common name. Google offered a lot of dead ends.

I also attempted to reach Jesse Faucette III without success.

B. Forrest Spink lives in Atlanta, Georgia. Contact him via email at bfspink@thomasmax.com

www.ingramcontent.com/pod-product-compliance
Lightning Source LLC
Chambersburg PA
CBHW051754040426
42446CB00007B/359